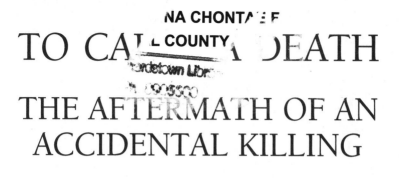

TO CAUSE A DEATH

THE AFTERMATH OF AN
ACCIDENTAL KILLING

KELLY CONNOR

CLAIRVIEW

*For my daughter Meegan, who taught me how to embrace life;
and for Margaret Healy, who taught me how to embrace death.*

Clairview Books
An imprint of Temple Lodge Publishing
Hillside House, The Square
Forest Row, RH18 5ES

www.clairviewbooks.com

Published by Clairview 2004

A catalogue record for this book is available from the British Library

ISBN 1 902636 55 4

Cover by Andrew Morgan Design
Typeset by DP Photosetting, Aylesbury, Bucks.
Printed and bound by Cromwell Press Limited, Trowbridge, Wilts.

Contents

A Note on the Author

Kelly Connor was born in the UK in 1954 and emigrated to Australia at age 11 with her family. At age 17, following the trauma described in *To Cause A Death*, she travelled across Australia and began a pattern that would become her signature: constant movement. She leads an unconventional, nomadic life that has taken her to many areas of both Australia and England. Her work experiences are as eclectic as her wanderings, including such varied fields as television production, organic vegetable gardening, political lobbying, administration, call centres, special needs education, and mothering. She has lived in England since 2001.

Introduction

In 1996, twenty-five years after causing the death of a pedestrian through negligent driving, I heard a radio interview describing an initiative to offer debriefing counselling to train and bus drivers who'd been involved in fatal collisions with pedestrians. At age seventeen, when I had my 'collision', no such debriefings existed, but after hearing the interview I knew that was what I still needed so I went in search of such a counsellor.

'The morning after the accident was pretty bad,' I said to the counsellor. 'At home, during the rush for everybody to get ready for work and school, nobody spoke a word about the horrors of the day before. I was rostered to start work at 8.30 am, which meant I was catching the same train as my mother. I don't remember whether we talked on our way to the station; perhaps we made small talk, but nothing more. On the train I felt better being surrounded by anonymous people, it eased the pressure of being amongst people who "knew". But while glancing at a newspaper held by another passenger I saw an article describing the accident. When I saw my name printed there, I instantly felt sick. A spinning, whirring sensation filled my head and I felt as though I was in a different dimension of time and space. It was horrible, I was screaming inside, but couldn't really be sure that I wasn't also screaming outside.'

We'd already had two sessions together and I was beginning to feel very comfortable about opening up to her. However, when I'd finished telling her about the train incident, she tilted her head to the side, leaned forward, sighed a little, then said, 'That's what we call a false memory. That incident couldn't have happened, it just feels like it did.'

'What do you mean?' I asked, in shock.

'Well, you were only seventeen at the time, which means the newspaper could not have identified you. Minors are legally protected from being publicly named so it couldn't have happened.'

'But it did,' I spluttered, ' I remember it so clearly.'

'I'm not saying you're making it up deliberately,' she said. 'It obviously feels very real to you, and so we need to work with those feelings, but we also need to be quite clear about what's real and what's not.'

'It was real, I know it was. It was as real as you and I sitting in this room.'

'Let me tell you how false memory works,' she said. 'You were probably sitting on the train that morning imagining how terrible it would be to see your name in the paper. This imagined fear became so strong that it actually began to feel real. Then, once you begin to feel something so intensely, it easily becomes imbedded as a memory. That's all that has happened to you. It's nothing to feel ashamed of, it's just part of the trauma. Don't worry,' she said smilingly, 'we can fix it.'

She was so unshakeably certain of her facts that I lost the power to defend myself. What if she was right? What else might I have imagined into my memory? Could I trust any part of my story to be accurate? There had been many times over the previous 25 years when seeking help in coming to terms with the enormous shame and guilt of causing some-body's death only led to disappointment, but this was the hardest failure of them all. It had simply never occurred to me that my memory of the events might be doubted, let alone declared false. The shock of her assertion was so profound that I was speechless. There was nothing else for me to do than rise from the chair, depart silently, and never return.

For the next six months I carried the shock of that encounter deep within me until eventually I realized that there was only one way to deal with the matter. I would have to put my memory to the test by turning to the newspaper archives. If my memory was right the archives would prove it. If not I'd have some serious mental health issues to confront.

This is an exact reproduction of the original article.

THE WEST AUSTRALIAN. APRIL 19 1971

Pedestrian (77) dies of injuries

A 77 year-old woman who was knocked down by a car in Victoria Park yesterday morning has died of injuries.

It was the only W.A. road death in the weekend and brought the State road toll for the year to 105, 18 fewer than the toll at the same time last year.

This year 23 pedestrians have been killed compared with 21 at the same time last year.

Miss Margaret Healy, of McMillan St, Victoria Park, was hit by a car when she was crossing Shepperton Road between Harper and Duncan Streets at about 8 am.

She died later in the casualty ward at the Royal Perth Hospital.

The car was driven by Brenda Connor (17), of Station St, Cannington.

The Victoria Park traffic branch has appealed to any witnesses, including the driver of a taxi seen close to the accident scene, to get in touch with him.

So far this year there have been 49 deaths on metropolitan roads and 56 in the country compared with 51 metropolitan and 72 country deaths at the same time last year.

As the article correctly reports, an elderly woman died a horrible, violent death; but what remains undescribed is the obliteration of self that I experienced in the awful moment of causing a person to die. My life wasn't taken from me, but my identity, my future, my past, and in many ways, my family, were lost to me as a consequence of this catastrophic moment in time.

It is impossible to know in advance the effect of trauma of this magnitude. If I'd been asked to speculate on how I might respond to this situation, I would have said something fatuous like, 'If it was a stranger who died, I would feel very sorry about it, but I'd just have to get on with my life. After all, what would be the point of upsetting myself over the death of somebody I didn't even know.'

I would also have rationalized the question of guilt with an easy dismissal, along the lines of: 'If you drive a car, or cross a road, you know there is always risk involved. These kinds of accidents can happen anywhere at anytime. So long as there is no malice or intent or gross negligence like drunkenness involved, then it's just an unfortunate accident. Get over it.'

However, my experience of the event proved to be completely different. I may not have incurred any physical injuries but my soul was gashed open and my mind was tormented beyond endurance. The journey of recovery has been long, arduous, lonely, and painful. Many of the people I turned to for help were unable to offer any, mostly because the nature of this trauma is too vast, too unknown, and too dreadful to contemplate. Few books are written on the subject, and few people speak about it.

During the thirty-year period that has passed since my accident, a further 16,071 pedestrians have died in Australia, as well as 51,709 British pedestrians, and 174,546 American pedestrians. Which means that in these three countries alone, as many as 242,326 drivers have experienced the trauma of knowing that they were directly involved in the death of another human being. Many of those drivers will be completely innocent of legal or criminal liability, yet the experience of knowing that they were the means by which the death of another person came about leaves an indelible mark upon the psyche.

This book is an attempt to describe the effect on my life of carrying this indelible mark. I will try to give a picture of how it feels to be responsible for causing the death of another human being. I will tell you of the horror, the guilt, the shame, the consequences, the tormenting questions, and ultimately the opportunity that it offered, or perhaps demanded, to reappraise my life and my values.

I have deliberately chosen to write entirely out of my own understanding and my own recollections of the events. However, this manner of writing necessarily restricts the scope of the story to one view only, my view. Please be aware that I am not intending to represent anybody else's experience of the events described. All the participants will have very individual, very different stories to tell. I don't know those stories, so I can only tell it through my own eyes, my own heart, and my own memory.

July 1965, a few weeks before departing for Sydney (I am centre)

1

January 1971

The deeply defining moments of life often, it seems to me, have an easily identifiable starting point. A moment at which one can look and say, 'There, that's where it all began.' This story begins on my seventeenth birthday when, as planned, I passed my driver's licence test. Obtaining my licence at the earliest possible moment was a goal I'd set myself some months before.

The first driving lesson had been incredibly exciting, partly in anticipation of the thrill of driving, and partly because it was something I was completely in charge of. I had set the goal, determined the time frame, studied the road rules, obtained the permit, and had booked and paid for the lessons out of my own wages. It was my project, my rite of passage, and my ticket to a liberated life.

None of my friends had cars and none of them shared my determination to get a driver's licence at the earliest possible moment. In fact it's probably fair to say that my approach to the subject was something of an aberration. It's also true to say that most of my zeal was motivated by wanting to upstage my older brother, Stephen.

Steve was older than me by two years, and although we had a close, loving and fun relationship, we had been locked in a game of one-upmanship for as long as I can remember. I was a Beatles fan, so he had to be a Stones fan; he supported Manchester United, so I declared allegiance to Man. City.

There was no malice involved, at least not any that I was conscious of, it was just our way of relating to each other. Perhaps it is not entirely true to say there was no malice though, for after all we did occasionally hurt each other, and I may have still been feeling a certain amount of resentment over a facial disfigurement that Steve had unwittingly inflicted on me five years before.

We had been sitting in the lounge room eating oranges when one of us threw some peel at the other; before long all the peel had been thrown so we moved onto other objects. Steve went into the bathroom and returned with a wet face cloth that he successfully aimed at my head. I was determined to also throw something wet at him but he was blocking the way to the bathroom, so I doubled back and headed for the kitchen. While I was at the sink wetting a tea towel he reappeared with another wet cloth and fired it in my direction. I ducked, laughing and squealing, only to forcefully collide my top front teeth against the corner of the stainless steel sink.

The force of the impact left a dent on the sink along with some white powder that was all that remained of the inner corner of my front left tooth that had broken off and pulverised. The right front tooth remained intact but had cracked in the centre from top to bottom. The pain was excruciating but my screaming was mostly due to the agonised fear of how hideous I surely looked − a fear compounded by seeing the look of shock and distress on Steve's face.

It was out of such fierce competitiveness between Steve and I that my licence plan was hatched. Steve had failed his first attempt at getting his licence, and out of his hurt and humiliation had made an off-hand comment about it being a signal that I shouldn't even bother thinking about it, let alone attempt it. In that instant, my mind was made up. I would get my licence at the first possible opportunity because it would give me an upper hand over Steve that could never be denied or bettered.

When my seventeenth birthday arrived, I was brimming with confidence. My lessons had gone well and my instructor had no doubts about my ability to pass the test. The test itself was unremarkable and unmemorable except for one small incident that would later prove to play a central role in the sorrow to come. We were on the home stretch, the test was almost over and I was feeling confident when the instructor noticed me glancing in the rear view mirror, and asked me how many cars were behind us. I gave the answer without hesitation but he then asked for the colour of the cars.

I was stumped, and momentarily shaken. Surely it couldn't be a requirement to know the colour of the cars travelling behind me, could it? I resisted the urge to peek in the mirror and took the gamble of saying the first colours that came to mind. Amazingly it was the right answer, but the incident left me with an unhealthy preoccupation about always knowing all the details of what was going on behind me.

The thrill of passing the test and receiving my licence was definitely the highlight of my young life; it proved beyond doubt that I was smarter and better than Steve, I couldn't wait to get home and watch him squirm. That evening we had a family dinner to celebrate my birthday. I don't remember the details of it but I do vividly recall the moment my father unexpectedly handed me his car keys and suggested that I drive over to visit my friend who lived in a nearby suburb. I say unexpectedly, because Steve had never been allowed to drive Dad's car and I simply presumed it would be the same with me. Steve was furious at this gesture, and doubtless deeply hurt, but I didn't care. I shook the keys under my brother's nose and flounced out.

Driving Dad's car on the very day that I passed my test was a coup that I had never even considered as a remote possibility. It skyrocketed me so far up the ladder of sibling rivalry that I knew Steve would never again catch me. My elation, however, was very short lived. About 5 seconds after leaving the driveway I came to the sickening realization that I had never driven in the dark before, nor had I driven alone before! I was scared stiff, so scared that I wanted to stop the car and go home. But that meant revealing my fear. And that meant losing my newly won victory over my brother, so I took a deep breath and kept driving.

Over the next couple of months I drove Dad's car more and more. He even had a spare key cut for me so that I could pick up the car from outside his workplace. He said it was silly to leave it sitting in the car park all day. Dad and I both worked rostered shifts, he was a bus driver and I was a telephonist at the GPO, so my free hours were often his working hours, giving me plenty of access to the car. I loved driving Dad's car. I loved the fact that he trusted me to drive it, and yes: I still loved the fact that Steve couldn't. Although by now Steve was vehemently declaring that he would never, under any circumstances, lower his standards to the point where he would be prepared to drive the old man's Toyota Crown.

How did this animosity come about? Firstly, at the time I didn't see it as animosity, it was just the way things were. I neither knew nor cared why we behaved the way we did, my only concern was for the outcome. And if the outcome meant that somebody had to lose for me to gain, then that's just the way it was, that was the natural order. After all, how was I to know that I had gained if there wasn't a subsequent loss elsewhere?

Our family had a naturally occurring fault line: Mum, Steve and Jayne, my younger sister, formed one alliance; while Dad and I formed the other. It wasn't that any of us disliked each other, quite the contrary, but it was just accepted that we fell into differing camps. At least, that was my experience of it, yet unbeknown to me there was resentment between Steve and Dad.

As a youngster, Steve had two distressing experiences with Dad of which I remained unaware for many years. They both occurred in my birthplace of Manchester, the city where we lived until emigrating to Australia in 1965. One involved an occasion when Dad had taken Steve, who was then seven or eight, to see Manchester United play soccer. At half-time Dad left Steve alone in the stands while he went to the bar to catch up with some friends. When he didn't return for the second half, Steve was worried but simply sat tight and waited. When the game was over, and Dad still hadn't returned, he started to cry. But his tears went unnoticed by hundreds of fans as they filed out past the frightened little boy. He was left alone in the empty, cold and rapidly darkening stands.

Dad, having found his mates in the bar and drunk a few ales with them, simply forgot that Steve was with him. In fact, it was not until he got home, worse for wear, that the awful truth dawned. He hightailed it back to Old Trafford with Mum's stinging, fearful anger ringing in his ears, and rescued his terrified son.

The other occasion again involved a father/son outing gone wrong. Dad and Steve had gone to see a boy's-own film about gladiators. Afterwards, at home, Steve was enthusing about the film's star, Steve Reeves, and was swooning over how much he 'loved' this man. Dad furiously turned on Steve, accusing him of behaving like a 'poofter'.

These two incidents were invisible in my account of family history, but they were the two occasions cited by Steve decades later as he sought for reasons to understand his imminent death from cancer at age 39. As a child, though, I was blissfully unaware of any underlying motives and dynamics that might have played into Dad's allegiance towards me. We all just played our roles and got on with it. For me, life was very sweet, and I felt enthusiastic about being alive. In fact my enthusiasm for life felt boundless when, at age eleven, Mum and Dad revealed that we were going to emigrate from our council estate in Manchester to the sunny climes of Sydney.

When we first arrived in Sydney we were placed into a migrant hostel at East Hills, 40 kms west of Sydney, in bushland. The site was a former army barracks consisting of scores of Nissen huts, tunnel-shaped and made of corrugated iron with a cement floor. The desolation and deprivation of the accommodation and the surroundings mortified our parents, but to me it was a grand adventure. The hut seemed exotic in its own peculiar way, but what really won me over was the enormous amount of freedom that living in the camp provided. Meal times were a prime example. Meals were served in a large cafeteria, with two or three choices for each course. This meant that kids who were big enough to take their own tray to the counter were largely freed from the tyranny of having to eat only what their mother provided. To be able to choose my own food was bliss; I don't recall any-thing about the quality or taste of the food, all that mattered was that the nexus between mother and food had been broken. Never again would I suffer the indignity of being forced to remain at the table until I had eaten my mother's offerings. It was truly liberating.

The other great delight was discovering the Australian bush. Steve and I roamed through the bush like explorers who had stumbled across the Garden of Eden. It was a dream world to a couple of kids who had grown up on a Manchester council estate deprived of much meaningful contact with nature save a few sparse street trees, a privet hedge and a patch of grass that passed for our garden. Amazingly, we felt no fear or anxiety about Australia's many venomous snakes or spiders. Fearlessness of the young perhaps.

After several months at East Hills, the authorities finally agreed to my parents' repeated requests to place us closer to the city, so we were transferred to Marrickville hostel in Sydney's southern suburbs. My parents were relieved to be back in civilization and closer to their workplaces, but Steve and I felt a little rueful about leaving the bush behind. However, our concerns were short-lived; the hostel was situated close to Australia's premier asset, the beach. The delights of the simple bush water hole that we so loved paled into insignificance beside the splendour of the grand Pacific Ocean and the abundant yellow sand.

In the new hostel our accommodation changed from individual Nissen huts to huge, long barracks that housed approximately 15–20 families and singles. We had three tiny rooms: one served as a bedroom for the three kids, one for our parents, and one as a lounge room. The bathroom was located at the end of the building and was shared with all the other occupants; it was primitive and inadequate, but at least it was now under the same roof, unlike the East Hills bathroom that involved a considerable walk through the elements. And, joy of joys, meals were again provided in the cafeteria.

I loved Sydney. We arrived just as the long summer holidays were starting, which meant Steve and I had loads of free time to ourselves. Our three favourite destinations were Maroubra beach, Luna Park, and La Perouse, the site of Captain Cook's landing in Australia in 1788. The beach always remained Steve's first love, but my affection for it waned dramatically after just a few weeks when I was dumped by a large wave. The terror of swirling around in the maelstrom of turbulent ferment was too much for me. I continued to love its splendour, but the power of the waves awed and daunted me. The quiet pleasures of the shallows and the rock pools became my preference.

There was no such reticence displayed at Luna Park, Sydney's famous fun fair situated on the edge of the magnificent harbour, just below the Sydney Harbour Bridge. The scary rides, the ghost train, and the house of horrors were all my favourites. My special favourite was the horror house you had to walk through, encountering all manner of ghosts, goblins, and skeletons along the way.

By far the greatest attraction to visiting Luna Park was the journey getting there. Our weekly pocket money was minimal, which meant we had to rely on wit and ingenuity instead. This involved avoiding bus fares by pretending to be part of another family group, jumping the turnstiles at the ferry terminal, and sneaking past the ticket collectors at the rides. It didn't always work. Many a time we had to trudge over the Harbour Bridge because we couldn't get on the ferry; but if you've seen the view from up there you'll know it wasn't much of a hardship.

Yet in many ways my favourite place was La Perouse, a strip of beach on the southern shores of the harbour. The tremendous history and significance of the place was irrelevant to me, in fact I'm not even sure if I knew it was the site of Cook's landing. What drew me there was the snake handler, and the Aborigines.

The snake handler was probably the most exotic, bewildering person I'd ever set eyes on. He stood in the centre of a low walled sandstone circle; at his feet rested half a dozen canvas sacks out of which he drew forth an astonishing range of reptiles. The scary thrills of Luna Park were nothing compared to the shock and fascination I experienced while watching the ease with which he allowed the disgusting, venomous creatures to wrap themselves around him. Occasionally he would carelessly allow a snake or two to slither away from his reach while he remained seemingly unaware of their escape until the shrill cries of the crowd alerted him. Often I feared for my life. The wall was very low, about one metre, and the snakes were very fast. Sometimes the urge to flee was immensely strong yet invariably I found myself rooted to the spot.

Some of the same sensations accounted for my fascination with the Aborigines at La Perouse. They seemed fearsome and foreboding with their strong, dark, distinctive faces. More often than not they sat clustered together, both shunning and shunned by the white visitors. I had neither the courage nor the interest to join them, but rarely could I take my eyes away. They represented something I had never encountered in England. It wasn't their skin colour – my best friend in Manchester had African parents so I was well used to dark skin – but something more primeval. They touched something in my psyche in the same way that the bush, the beach, and the wildlife of Australia had touched me. Their presence somehow woke me up, opened me up, forcing me to become aware of my surroundings and myself in a new way.

Sydney had provided one excitement after another, at least Stephen and I saw it that way, but it seems our parents hadn't. After only a year, my parents announced that we were on the move again, this time from Sydney to Perth, overland across the Nullabor desert. One day Dad arrived home and asked me to get something from the car that he had forgotten, but when I went outside the car was nowhere to be seen. Worriedly, I went back inside to tell him the bad news, only to find he and my mother grinning inanely. The keys in my hand were for a different car, a Holden station wagon, which, said my parents, was going to take us across the continent. Thus was the announcement of our imminent departure made. I didn't mind at all, it was just a further extension of a marvellous adventure to me. We had crossed the world, and were now about to cross the world's largest island continent. What more could an adolescent ask for?

The first part of our journey, the drive to Adelaide, was on reasonably good roads; but once we reached Ceduna, some 400 kms west of Adelaide, the sealed road ended. We now faced a 1500 km drive on a dirt road across the Nullabor desert. We all had some degree of anxiety about the desert crossing, but by way of a soothing 'treat' beforehand, Mum had booked us into a Ceduna motel so that we could have a good night's sleep and a proper shower and breakfast before embarking upon the dusty crossing. It was a good plan and we were all looking forward to it. However, there was one major flaw. Nobody had considered whether the normal facilities of life would be available in a town that exists on the edge of a desert. Ceduna has a hot, dry climate, hence not much rainfall, but being situated close to the coastline of the Great Australian Bight gave it a ready supply of water – the vast Southern Ocean.

Our discovery of the salt water supply occurred in three simultaneous, but different ways. I was in the shower, complaining about the lack of lather in the shampoo, Steve was complaining about the taste of the water while cleaning his teeth, while Mum and Dad were spitting out the cups of tea they had been eagerly looking forward to. Initially, we simply couldn't comprehend that we were encountering salt water. It was a concept too far fetched for our English sensibilities, but when the truth dawned we were horrified. What's worse, we were deprived of the very goal we were seeking; a clean, refreshed feeling. Instead, our skin was sticky and our hair looked like straw; we were not happy campers. Next morning we set out on our journey feeling less than enthusiastic about the inevitable discomfort to our skin of the combined effect of salt, sweat, dust and heat.

We had now been travelling for almost a week and the novelty was wearing thin; yet despite this I still felt a thrill of excitement about the romance of a desert crossing. The obvious question that arises is, how did a bunch of Poms born and raised in one of the world's great industrialized cities manage to find the concept of crossing a desert on a dusty unsealed road to be romantic rather than repellent? I can't speak for other members of my family, but for me the crossing experience was a deeply profound awakening of consciousness.

Hour upon hour I looked out at the vast expanse of land that stretches to the horizon on its full 360-degree vista. My eyes drank in the isolation, the complete stillness, and the utter forsakenness of an environment where neither humans, fauna, nor flora choose to live. Above, the relentless blue sky and the blazing sun beat down upon this unimaginably aged piece of earth. And all the while five foreign interlopers crowded inside a metal capsule continued to push onwards towards they knew not what. It was exhilarating to acknowledge ourselves capable of achieving this mighty enterprise, but more importantly it opened up an awareness in me of new possibilities, new realities. I'm certain that destiny required me to cross this desert so that its vastness and steadfastness would provide me with a counter-balance to the shocking experiences that still lay ahead.

The journey to Perth brought many changes in its wake, not the least of which was the effect upon my education. My schooling ended when I was fourteen years old, not because I left school early but because I'd twice been elevated a grade, which meant my class peers were all turning sixteen, the usual leaving age.

Nobody in my family, from either side, had been to university so choosing a profession was never even considered let alone discussed. Nevertheless, there was one job that seemed to me to stand out above all others. I wanted to be an international airhostess so that I could travel the world. Unfortunately though, it was already clearly apparent that I wouldn't meet the height requirement so I had to set my sights elsewhere.

The first job that came my way was working in a florist shop. Floral arranging appealed to the romantic in me, but romantic notions about being surrounded by fragrant flowers soon evaporated. My first task was to accompany the senior florist to a variety of offices in the city; we carried a large amount of fresh flowers to replace the dead and dying ones from the week before. It was my job to do the carrying of the fresh flowers, to remove and dispose of the old flowers, and to wash the smelly vases. After a couple of hours of this I was very pleased when advised that we were heading back to the shop. However, I was then informed that my next task was to take a funeral wreath to the cemetery, on the bus! I did as I was instructed, but after delivering the wreath I vowed never to go back to the shop; thus my first job lasted only a few hours. My second job as a receptionist in a small city office was better, but seemed mostly to consist of making cups of tea for the two partners.

Then, at the grand age of fifteen and a half, I started my third job as a telephonist with the General Post Office (GPO) in Perth. I'm not sure what it was that appealed to me about the job, something about the universal nature of communication I suppose, but it proved to be a blessing. For the first time in my life I felt myself to be in an environment where my capacities were not only meaningfully challenged, but also where they were actually put to some useful purpose. The task of assisting people to engage with the emerging world of telecommunications was one that I relished.

The Perth telephone exchange of 1970 was of the cords and plugs variety, which consisted of huge boards that had plugholes and lights on the upper vertical board, and cords, switches and lights on the lower horizontal board. When a call was incoming a bulb would light up under the plug, requiring the rear cord to be placed into the plug to answer it. Then, to connect the caller to another number, the corresponding front plug would be inserted into another outgoing socket from which the number could be dialled. This was all pretty straightforward for a single call, but each operator had twenty incoming lines to manage which usually meant that one call was being connected while simultaneously another one was being answered, a further one was being monitored for progress, and yet another one was being disconnected.

There was plenty of manual dexterity required along with good visual and verbal skills. I thrived on the challenge of having to think, listen, act, observe and speak all at the same time. All long distance calls were connected through an operator, and all connections were recorded on hand-written dockets that were then manually collated in preparation for manual pricing and sorting. In other words, it was a busy, satisfying, multi-skilled job.

We worked in four long rows of 'cords and plugs boards', which seated about twenty operators in each row. All operators were female, ranging from school leavers to middle aged (compulsory retirement for women was 55), and we were sternly watched over by women monitors who ruled the floor with firm discipline. As well as enjoying the work, I also enjoyed the all-female environment. There was something very nurturing and nourishing about the energy that was generated amongst the women, and I was particularly blessed to have the privilege of watching the emerging consciousness of feminism amongst my co-workers, which, of course, also fed my own emerging consciousness.

Some aspects of the feminist movement excited me enormously; others left me a little bemused. For instance, the idea that women should break out of the home and join the workforce seemed perfectly natural to me; my mother had been working outside the home for as long as I could remember. Whether she worked when I was a baby I couldn't say; but certainly she was working soon after my sister Jayne was born. How well Steve and I remembered an awful night when both Mum and Dad were working an evening shift and we were left to look after Jayne. She was still a small baby, which meant Steve was seven and I was five. She cried and cried, and was clearly unwell. I being the younger one didn't

really take much of it in; but Steve was feeling quite distressed
– with good reason; Jayne was later diagnosed with whoop-
ing cough!

Mum was an intelligent young woman who probably could
have gone a long way in other circumstances, but being born
into 1930s working class Manchester meant that she finished
school at age 12 and began an unskilled working life. She had
worked in various shops, factories, and offices throughout
her four and a half decades of employment, and although she
had opportunities for advancement and recognition, she
refused to take them.

She was the second youngest child in a family of six; the
last three children, all girls, were considerably younger than
the first three. Indeed so great was the age difference that
when the war started the younger three were sent away as
child evacuees, while her brothers went to war and the eldest
sister watched her husband go to war.

Being a child evacuee was a deeply traumatic experience
for my mother, Patricia. She was nine years old when, along
with her elder sister, Wynne, and younger sister, Vera, she
was wrenched from home and family and, along with a group
of other children, sent to a country village. She found herself
herded into a village hall where local residents were waiting
to handpick the children they wanted to take home. Nobody
wanted to take three sisters, so it was decided to split them
up, keeping the older and younger sisters together, but
leaving Patricia alone.

As if the separation from her sisters wasn't traumatic
enough, she then found herself to be the only child whom
nobody had picked to take home. She attributes this to a
disfiguring accident she had a few years earlier when she hit
her head at the swimming pool, causing her left eye to turn

inwards. To correct the turned eye, she had to wear very thick glasses, which left her feeling, and to her mind, looking, very ugly.

After everybody had left the hall, the evacuation organizer took Patricia from house to house cajoling people to take the pathetic little creature into their homes. Many refused, but eventually a woman relented and took Pat in. But when her husband arrived home that evening he fiercely objected. So, the next day, the rounds of houses began again. This time an elderly lady, who lived in a rather large, grand house took her in. Both the house and the occupant were deeply intimidating to Patricia, and to make matters even worse her first evening in the house was completely terrifying. She slept in a large four-poster bed in a very large room; the foreignness of it was excruciating enough, but on the wall was something that utterly scared the wits out of her: a large portrait. Patricia had never seen a portrait; indeed she didn't even know such a thing existed. She lay in bed shivering with fear and dread about the person who looked down at her watching her every move. Fortunately, during her mother's first visit, it became clearly apparent that Patricia wasn't coping so she accompanied her mother back home to Manchester.

My mother is a strong-minded, independent person; I certainly didn't equate her with the picture of a submissive wife chained to the house, but unbeknown to me she had been suffering a deep unhappiness for many years. Like most adolescents, I was utterly unconcerned about the emotional welfare of my parents; they didn't impose any information about themselves upon me, and I didn't seek any. However, when I was fourteen, Dad went away for a few months to work at the lucrative iron ore mines in the north of the state. Later, we were told it was really a trial separation. It was a bit of a jolt to hear that, but it didn't have any real emotional impact because he came back before we had even realized what was happening.

My life was too busy and too much fun to bother about other people's lives. I loved the freedom of being a working girl; buying clothes was one of my favourite pastimes and the other was going out at night. My workplace greatly assisted participation in these two activities by allowing me to choose the afternoon shift, 3pm–11pm, as my preference. This shift not only provided higher wages, it meant I was part of a group of girls who went straight out to a club after work, danced until 3am, slept all morning, then went to work ready to do it all again the next night.

Mum didn't like me being out late – we had been having arguments about it since before I left school. Eventually she came to accept it, partly because it was just too tiring to keep up the objections, but also because it became clear that I wasn't likely to get myself into trouble. I rarely drank anything other than water; alcohol tasted too disgusting to spend my wages on, and in truth, the main attractions for me were music and dancing. I loved to spend hours on the dance floor and I quickly discovered that alcohol impaired rather than enhanced the experience.

Boys weren't an attraction either; I did enjoy knowing they were watching me on the dance floor, but my biggest thrill came out of rejecting their advances when they wanted to dance with me or buy me a drink. I'm not sure why this came about, but perhaps it had something to do with hearing Steve and his mates discussing their evening exploits. It always seemed as though their greatest derision was reserved for the girls who responded warmly to them.

There was one boy though who got through my defences,

Joe. He was a couple of years older than me, a good-looking boy of Yugoslav immigrant parents who was studying law at university. We met when I was sixteen in my favourite haunt, The Waldorf Club. I liked him because his only apparent interest was in talking to me. He didn't want to dance with me, or get me drunk, or get into my pants, or marry me. We spent hours debating the hotspots of the world: Vietnam, the cold war, the space race; and most especially, we discussed the ethics of criminal law. Joe's ambition was to be Australia's top criminal lawyer, a goal I scathingly dismissed as abhorrent. I'd tell him there was no honour in defending crooks and murderers; he would reply that society's greatest single achievement was the principle that everyone is innocent until proven guilty. 'Having the opportunity to defend and protect that principle is the highest honour of all,' he would say. 'Not,' I hotly retorted, 'if it means a single guilty person goes free.'

Our debates were enormously satisfying to me and although Joe was a very attractive boy with lots of admirers (including himself), he was not boyfriend material — not in my eyes anyway. Sometimes I did wonder whether we should get together, but then he would display some grotesque example of chauvinism and put me off completely. The worst occasion happened one evening when he had suggested that we watch television together at his house. He still lived at home so I knew it would be safe, but I also wondered if this was his way of saying he wanted me to meet his parents.

When I arrived he briefly and casually introduced me to his Mum who was sitting at the kitchen table; he then took me straight into the lounge room. After a few minutes he bellowed for his mother to come into the room. His tone and volume surprised me; after all it was a small house and she was only in the next room, but I surmised that he was inviting her in to watch the programme. When she entered the room, he instructed her to change the TV channel, which she did and then she immediately left the room without comment. 'Do you do that often?' I asked. When he confirmed it was normal for him to treat his mother this way I shouted my disapproval and departed.

Strident exchanges between Joe and I didn't damage our friendship; in a funny way they strengthened it. For me, they affirmed my burgeoning sense of self, my need to work out what my thoughts and feelings were in relation to the world. They also gave me scope to test out how far I could push my views and opinions. Joe had a good mind, a quick mind; he forced me to think on my feet, to defend a thought that I had never been aware of until it formed itself out of my mouth. Sometimes I didn't like him; but I liked who I was in his presence.

My life was truly as happy and fulfilled as I had ever known it to be, and amazingly it was getting more exciting day by day, for in only three weeks' time I was due to begin a working holiday around Australia with three girls from work. Eve was the only one of the group who was a special friend of mine, the other two I hardly knew, but in one of her exuberant moments she had convinced or perhaps steamrolled the other two into asking me to go with them. Eve was a year or so older than I was and a year or two younger than the others – she was one of life's natural rebels, irrepressible, daring, joyous, and reckless, which was why I liked her so much.

The plan was to catch a train across the continent from Perth to Melbourne; then to hitchhike from Melbourne up to northern Queensland where waitressing jobs were waiting at Green Island resort. I was astonished that they wanted me to join what I considered an elite group; naturally I said yes, but I didn't really believe that my parents would give me permission to go. Amazingly, they did, even though we had given only very short notice of our intention to depart.

My happiness felt eternal. I could not, did not, envisage anything intruding upon my joy. Yet three months after passing my driving test, destiny was waiting to meet me in a deeply shocking and horrible encounter, which as though in deliberate counterpoise to its terribleness came on a beautifully mild, sunny autumn morning. It was the Sunday after Easter, and it was my sister Jayne's twelfth birthday.

April 1971, Perth

2

Sunday 18 April 1971

As is usual for an autumn morning in Perth, the sky was blue and the air had a hint of coolness to it, but the warmth was not far away. On this beautiful Sunday morning I was rostered to work the 8 am to 12 noon shift, which would normally mean that I'd take Dad's car. However, Dad and Mum were planning to take Jayne out for a birthday treat later that morning, so the plan was for Dad to drive me to work. Yet when the morning arrived, Dad decided he was too tired, so we arranged instead that I should take the car to work and then later, after a lie-in, my parents and sister would catch the train to my workplace and we would all go together to Jayne's birthday outing.

It was an ordinary enough decision at the time, but with the benefit of hindsight it now seems as though fate had its hand on my shoulder from this first innocent moment to the final tragic outcome.

After a quick breakfast I got into the car, reversed out of the driveway and found myself facing the opposite direction to where I intended to go! I was slightly bemused by this lapse of concentration, but after a moment's consideration I decided to go with the flow, realizing that I could take advantage of the quiet Sunday morning traffic to travel the main highway to work rather than my usual backstreet route. This added a few extra minutes to the journey but I wasn't pressed for time because I had left a little earlier than usual. I cruised along,

enjoying the new experience of travelling a road that previously I had been somewhat unnerved by. But after ten
minutes or so, I found myself turning off the highway and
back onto the route I usually travelled. Again, I was a bit
bemused by this because I hadn't consciously decided to
change routes, it just happened; and uncharacteristically, I
again just submitted and continued my journey, smiling at
the weirdness of it.

I was now back on a very familiar road with almost no
other traffic, so was feeling very relaxed. I approached part of
the road that had a fairly steep hill to climb, and had begun to
press down the accelerator when I noticed a taxi pull up at the
crossroads at the top of the hill. It occurred to me that the
driver might pull out in front of me because up until that very
morning he would have had right of way. The road rules gave
right of way to any vehicle entering traffic from the right, so
normally I would have had to stop to allow him to turn in
front of me. However a new rule was now in place that gave
me right of way because I was travelling on a designated
priority road and he was entering from a side street.

I fixed my attention on him, ready to take evasive action
should it be needed. In truth though, my diligence was largely
due to the sudden realization that an accident would ser-
iously interfere with my holiday plans, so I poured all my
attention into ensuring that I was not going to get into a tangle
with the taxi. He didn't pull out, but after passing him my
attention was still so fixed on him that even as I passed
beyond the intersection I continued watching him in my rear-
view mirror. It was only when I saw him leave the corner and
turn behind me that I became aware I hadn't eased up on the
accelerator even though I was now well over the crest of the
hill.

When I looked forwards, I saw an elderly lady in a green suit directly in front of me who was two-thirds of the way across the road on a pedestrian crossing. I immediately hit the brakes, causing her to look up in terrified horror. With absolutely no hope of success, she tried to outrun me.

When she first stepped onto the crossing I would have been at the bottom of the hill completely out of her sight. Yet now, with her crossing almost complete I was barrelling towards her at high speed. Did our eyes meet? I don't know. Sometimes I imagine that they did but I don't usually allow myself to dwell on the moments immediately before impact. I remember slamming on the brakes, and I remember the sensation the squealing tyres made, but curiously I don't recall the actual noise.

The noise of the impact is also lost to me. I only remember the intense silence that followed it. I sat in that silence for what seemed an eternity but which must only have been seconds. I sat wondering whether I had only imagined the woman on the crossing. I couldn't see her. I couldn't hear her. Maybe it hadn't actually happened. I was on the brink of convincing myself that I should just leave when the taxi pulled up in front of me and the driver got out and ran over. He motioned at me to open the window but I just stared blankly unable to move. He shouted through the window that he had radioed for an ambulance. He also told me that he had a passenger and had to leave.

As he drove away his words about an ambulance filtered through my brain and I realized that I really must have hit the woman. At that I began to panic; my hands, arms, and legs became tingling and shaky. My breathing became short and erratic as I contemplated the scene that awaited me outside the car. Gruesome images of blood and gore pressed into my mind, but as terrible as they were, another part of me was taking charge. I remembered hearing about the need to keep accident victims warm, and at the same instant I recalled that there was a blanket on the back seat from the drive-in movie I went to with my family the night before. I got the blanket and walked around the side of the car to cover her: she was lying on her stomach unmoving, not far from the front left tyre. Surprisingly there was no blood, or at least none that I allowed myself to see. I was relieved that I didn't have to look at her face, or have her look at mine.

As I covered her, a van with surfboards on top pulled alongside and stopped. One of the four young men inside got out, picked up the woman's handbag and glasses from the road and placed them gently beside her. Without saying a word he then got back into the van and they left. 'Please don't leave me alone,' my mind wailed as they drove away. I slumped against the car near to where she was lying but I couldn't bring myself to look at her, not even to see whether she was breathing.

Just then, a young woman in a nurse's uniform appeared, I presumed she was with the ambulance and was surprised that I hadn't noticed their arrival, but it turned out that she was just driving past on her way to work. She quickly examined the woman, assured me that she only had a broken leg, explained that she was late for work, and left. For the third time I was abandoned to deal with this nightmare alone. Despite the assurances of the nurse, it seemed clear to me that something terrible was in the air. Why else did everybody keep leaving?

Shortly afterwards the police arrived, followed almost immediately by the ambulance. Then amazingly the scene was suddenly swarming with people. It was almost as though they had been hiding in the bushes waiting for the authorities to arrive. Possibly they came from the Catholic Church situated directly across the road. I later learned that that was where Margaret Healy had just come from.

A police officer drew me aside to ask my name and address, positioning me so that my back was facing the ambulance officers attending the woman. His kind intentions were interrupted by an aggressive on-looker accusing me of being too young to drive, demanding to know whether I held a driving licence. The policeman's response was to place me in the back seat of Dad's car and close the door while he spoke to the man.

After the ambulance left, I was beckoned from Dad's car and placed in the front seat of the police van to be driven to the police station. I recall feeling really surprised that another police officer drove my Dad's car to the station rather than asking me to do it, but, more disturbingly, I also realized at that moment that my thinking capacity had somehow changed. I was aware of feeling distinctly odd. My brain felt somehow numb, as though it had stopped working. It was as though my faculties of speech and movement were on auto-pilot: they were still functioning reasonably normally, but I couldn't feel myself participating or actively engaging.

I had no idea what was awaiting me at the police station, and I'm not sure if I even thought much about it because I was assuming that they were taking me to the cells. Though in truth it didn't really matter to me what they were doing. I was incapable of any form of useful thought or reflection; they could have been taking me for immediate execution and I wouldn't have uttered a single objection. I was just grateful that they were making all the decisions and asking none of me.

When we arrived at the station I was taken into a small office and given a chair beside one of the two desks. One of the officers sat at the same desk, in front of a typewriter, while the other officer sat further away but still close by. They made me a cup of tea and then began the process of taking my statement, which went unremarkably until we came to the question of the speed I was travelling.

I couldn't say accurately, but admitted that I must have been travelling very fast due to not releasing the accelerator after climbing the hill.

'Yes, but how fast?' he pressed.

'Well, perhaps 45 mph (72 kph) or thereabouts, I suppose,' I said, hanging my head in shame.

'Do you know the speed limit?' he asked.

'Yes, 35 mph (55 kph).'

'Then how fast were you travelling?'

'Probably 45 mph,' I repeated, after some confused hesitation.

He sighed and then gently repeated, 'What is the speed limit?'

'35 mph' I said, haltingly.

'Then how fast were you travelling?' he repeated.

I sat silently, looking from one policeman's face to the other. They both avoided eye contact, preferring to fiddle with objects in front of them. I didn't know what to say. Were they inviting me to lie about the speed I was travelling, or were they trying to determine my moral standing. My numbed mind couldn't cope with weighing the odds, so not caring about the consequences, or being even able to contemplate them, I took a gamble and said, '35 mph.'

'Good' he said, and typed my answer.

Another area of critical importance was the question of

whether the woman was on the pedestrian crossing at the time of impact.

'Think very carefully before you answer this question,' the policeman cautioned.

'Well, yes, she must have been,' I said.

'Can you state with absolute certainty that she was definitely on the crossing?'

'She must have been.'

'Did you actually see her standing on the crosswalk?'

I lowered my eyes, 'No, I was too close to her to see much of anything.'

'Then can you be absolutely certain that she was on the crossing?'

'No,' I finally conceded, 'I can't say that for certain.' I knew that she was but it seemed too much effort to try to work out why the police didn't want me to say it, so I just submitted.

When the statement was complete, one of them phoned the hospital to check on the woman's condition, which was reported as critical, but stable. I was then asked if I wanted to phone anybody; I briefly thought about phoning Joe, my legal student friend, to ask him to get me released but I knew I didn't deserve it, so just shook my head, no. When they then indicated that they were going to take me home, I almost cried with relief. I wasn't going to the cells after all.

Again, one of them drove Dad's car while I travelled in the front of the police van. It was around 9 am by the time we arrived and my parents were still indulging in their Sunday morning lie-in. They were called unceremoniously to the front door and greeted by the sight of their daughter flanked by two policemen.

The police officers gestured for me to go inside while they stood on the doorstep telling the news to Mum and Dad. The front door opened directly into our small lounge room, placing me only a few paces away from where everyone else was standing. Jayne was also sitting in the lounge room, listening to the doorstep conversation while looking at me with a mixture of great fear and deep concern. It wasn't long before she convulsed into sobs of tears, partly out of sympathy for my plight, and partly out of recognition that her special day was ruined. I turned away, shamed to the core that her day would now always carry this taint upon it.

The doorstep exchange between the police and my parents was short but revealing. My mother only wanted to know the condition of the woman, to which the police replied that the situation was still unclear. My father didn't say anything much, but was advised by the officers to change the balding front right tyre before the accident investigation squad came to inspect the car.

As soon as the police left, my mother announced that we were going to the hospital. I started to protest, saying that I was all right. She looked startled. 'Not for you,' she said, 'I want to know if the woman needs our help.' I received no hugs or kisses, no words of comfort to assure me of my continued acceptance within the family, no questions about my welfare, and no opportunity to ask for or to receive forgiveness. Instead, within ten minutes my parents and I were back in the car driving to the hospital, leaving the birthday girl home alone, shocked and distressed.

Thankfully Dad drove the highway route, avoiding the accident scene. However, on arrival at the hospital he opted to wait in the car, leaving Mum and I to go in together. As we walked towards the emergency entrance, the first person we encountered was one of the police officers who had taken me home. He asked whether I was all right, obviously presuming my welfare to be the reason for our visit. My mother dismissed his question saying she wanted to visit the woman to see if she needed any assistance. The policeman showed us to the emergency waiting room, saying he would return shortly with news.

A few minutes later, an elderly man accompanied by a middle-aged couple entered the waiting room and sat directly in front of us. They and we were the only people in the waiting room, they in the front row of seats, Mum and I just to the side of them on an adjacent bench seat. From their conversation it quickly became apparent that they were related to the woman. I sat in frozen terror, desperately wishing that the earth would open up and swallow me. My mother sat still and silent, giving no indication of whether she was aware of who they were or what they were discussing. 'Please, please don't say anything,' I silently pleaded to Mum, terrified she might say something that would reveal who I was.

A mercifully short time later the police officer came back. Without even glancing at my mother or me he strode over to the people sitting in front and escorted them down a corridor. I began to relax a little, believing that when the police officer came back he would tell us that her family was with her so we could leave. A few minutes later he did return. He sat down beside me, and with more gentleness than I would have considered possible, told me that the woman had died.

My head filled with a whirring noise, one that came from within me not from without, and I felt as though I no longer occupied the same time and space as my mother and the policeman. I could see them and hear them, but somehow they were no longer real. I instantly knew that the world and my place in it had irrevocably changed. I must have looked as sick as I felt because the policeman started to walk away, telling my mother that he was going to get a doctor. She stopped him, saying it wouldn't be necessary. Instead she indicated that we were to leave, so, ignoring his protest we walked quickly and silently to the car where she brusquely informed Dad of what had happened. On the drive home, Mum instructed Dad to drive past the accident scene. 'Well at least there are skid marks,' she muttered.

The rest of the day was strained and terrible for all of us. Jayne cried inconsolably for the loss of her special day, and perhaps for the loss of the special esteem in which she had held me. Dad was stunned and shaken that his generosity to me had resulted in such horror, a horror in which I suspected he felt himself to be complicit. Mum was stern, ashen faced, and utterly determined that this event wouldn't be allowed to change or influence our lives. Her determination was such that when she had come into the lounge room to find Dad asking me to describe what had happened, she issued an ultimatum that we were never ever to speak about it. My brother Steve had gone away surfing with some friends for the weekend, so he wouldn't find out until he got home late that evening.

For me, a collage of memories remains from that day. Standing in the shower crying. Needing to have lots of showers. Avoiding eye contact. Silence. Cups of sweet tea. The shock of hearing the accident described on the evening news. Mum telling me to cease driving until after the investigation; and Dad submitting to my mother's instruction not to talk to me about the accident. But perhaps the most painful memory is of lying awake in bed waiting for Steve to return home in the hope that he would know the right words to say which would make my world seem normal again. When he finally did come home, I heard muffled voices in the lounge room and knew that my parents had waited up to tell him the news. I fully expected him to come immediately into my room. He didn't. He went straight to bed.

3

April–May 1971

On the third evening after the accident, just prior to the moment of falling asleep, I experienced the sickening sensation of my head seeming to cleave apart; then, almost instantaneously I was violently snatched from my body and cast into unimaginable terror. I was thrown into a place that was like a darkened cavern or ravine. On either side of me, towering high above my head, was a massed collection of beings engaged in a boiling fury of argument and counter-argument about spiritual law and consequence. I listened petrified, only to realize with dread that the argument was about which of these beings had the right to claim ownership over my soul. Almost as soon as coming to this realization I was banished from the scene and hurled back into my body, shaking, sweating, and in a state of such utter terror that it was impossible for me to make any sense of what had happened.

But it wasn't finished. The next evening, again just at the moment of falling asleep, I was hauled back to the same darkened ravine where the same court of fearsome beings continued their battle. This second occurrence was also over very quickly; no sooner had I begun to gather my wits than I was again cast out, as though the only purpose in having me there was to ensure that I knew the trial was happening. Nothing had been asked of me and no acknowledgement of my presence was given. This time though, the terror that rose to meet me as I was flung back into my body was the fear that being summoned to this unearthly court was an event that was going to happen again and again.

At first I did all in my power to either deny or resist this process, but I soon began to realize that resistance to the summons was futile. I found myself almost unwittingly preparing for these evening encounters by bracing myself for the event, which, in turn, meant that I arrived in a better state. At this early stage I still didn't know who the beings were, nor did I have a good visual image of them; I only ever experienced them as a massed collection of energies, but it seemed from the way they occupied different sides of the ravine that they surely represented opposing forces, though distinguishing differences between the two forces was at first extremely difficult.

Both were so exceptionally frightening that the prospect of being claimed by either of these groups of beings was unendurable. One side, though, clearly expressed themselves with far more severity than the other, causing me to shrink away from them even more. My guilt was never an issue in this court; its certainty was clearly beyond dispute, the only purpose of this trial was to decide the consequence of the guilt, to resolve which force I now belonged to. This was done by conducting a rigorous assessment of where my spiritual allegiances lay; and no, that didn't mean examining my religious affiliations. It was a much harsher test than that. It meant having all the events of the day observed, scrutinized, and assessed to see which spiritual realm my behaviour belonged to.

Each evening, the two sides would examine every aspect of my behaviour throughout that day, up to and including my arrival at the court. During this process I learnt that spiritual courts judge earthly actions by very different criteria than our legal courts or religious institutions. I learnt that every judgement would rest on the determination of my motive, on what intention lay behind each action. Every day I had to weigh and measure each thought, comment, and activity to determine which of the spiritual forces would use it as evidence that night. I quickly learnt that any 'good' actions that arose from selfish motives would invoke a fierce response of rebuke from the severe beings; whereas the other beings seemed to become strengthened or emboldened by such false 'goodness' and would encourage me to continue with such behaviour.

The severe beings were totally focused on exposing every aspect of the hidden, unconscious parts of myself. They were terrible and formidable in their fierce insistence on truth in all things: their relentlessness was without pity. The other beings, by comparison, seemed at times to be almost courteous, yet as the trial continued they revealed a distinct inability to remain constant. Their fierceness easily slipped into rage; their love always involved deception; and their truth relied on flexible interpretations.

Working out who or what these beings represented was something of a slow process. Religion had rarely been discussed in my family so I had grown up largely unconcerned about the presence or existence of the forces of good and evil, but I came to realize that these forces are the beings we call angels and demons. And though initially it was the angels who terrified me the most, it became apparent that their very fierceness also contained unswerving love and acceptance.

Discovering the identities of the forces changed the dynamics markedly. I was no longer petrified into frozen silence during these evening encounters but instead found myself more and more able to speak up in my own defence. My terror of these encounters eased a little once I began to make sense of the importance of motive and the discovery that what we do in the world holds little significance compared to why we do it. Yet truthfully scrutinizing our motives is no easy thing. Time and again I was taken to task for failing to acknowledge the selfish or mindless or careless influences that determined my decisions, though with each passing night it became transparently clear that despite all their severity the angels had no desire to relinquish me to the demons. Rather, they were intent upon ensuring that the demons could make no rightful claim over me. Amid these realizations I reclaimed my self-confidence to the point that, quite spontaneously, I heard myself announce one night that I was no longer prepared to participate in these spiritual trials. 'My life belongs to neither of you. It is mine alone, and I claim it back!' Surprisingly, my demand was immediately acceded to: the trial ceased forthwith. How long the whole process took, or how many times I visited the ravine, is impossible to say, though it feels as if it had been a nightly event over a period of two to three weeks.

The cessation, along with my assumption that the dark forces had not yet won the right to claim my soul, should have brought some relief, but it didn't. At the time I didn't have the capacity to reflect on what had happened, it was all just part of the nightmare. I knew that everything about the experience was real and actual, but equally I knew that I mustn't speak to anyone about my experiences. Partly because it would be too easy for people to declare me mad, but mostly because of a deep sense of knowing that this trial was right and necessary.

Part of that knowing must have stemmed from an experience I had as a young child when I met my guiding angel. I was about six years old when I awoke one night to find an angelic being in my room. I was deeply frightened by this and called out for my mother. After several shrill calls she came into my room in rather a grumpy but concerned manner after obviously being awoken from a deep sleep. But to my amazement, she walked right past the shimmering white figure, completely unaware of its presence. When Mum asked me why I had called her, I was so dumbfounded I lamely said that I wanted to go to the toilet. Exasperated, she carried me past the glorious shimmering light to the toilet, and then she carried me past it again on returning me to bed. Transfixed I watched her pass for a fourth time as she left my room to return to hers. By now my fear had evaporated and I asked the angel why it was that my mother hadn't seen. The angel replied, 'You have been given a picture of your destiny. It is your fate to see, hear and experience things that others cannot or will not. It will become your destiny to find a way to bridge our two worlds.'

Any connection between this childhood angelic visitation and the horror of the evening trials was completely lost on me at the time. My mental and emotional faculties were still in a type of short-circuit or meltdown, making it impossible to connect any threads together. I was still experiencing the sense of existing in a different state of time and space to everyone else, which felt like being in an out-of-sync movie that I couldn't turn off. It also was becoming apparent that there were two distinct thought processes now working through me. One was the shocked, frightened self; the other was a calm, steady, reassuring voice that spoke to me at the most unlikely times. This was not an external voice, more like a spoken thought whose voice, though unfamiliar to me, felt deeply known. Perversely, it was the very calmness of this

voice that spooked me so much. Another disturbing awareness took the form of a heightened sensitivity to energy forces
that were all around me. I could feel the presence of invisible
beings and could inwardly hear an unearthly hum that
seemed to permeate through everything. In part, this sensitivity arose both from the demands of the trials and of the
shifting thought patterns, but it was also due to the daily
torment of knowing that I had caused a death. A torment that
was all-encompassing, all-pervading, and always, always
present.

The morning after the accident, during the hurry for us all
to get ready for work and school, not a word about the accident passed between any of us. Unusually, I was rostered to
start work at 8.30 am, which meant that I was catching the
same train as my mother. Did we talk on our way to the
station? I don't remember; perhaps we made small talk, but
nothing more. Once on the train I felt marginally comforted
by the crush of anonymous people, which eased the relentless
pressure of being amongst people who 'knew'. Then, while
mindlessly casting my eye over the newspaper held by the
man in front of me, I caught sight of an article in the morning
newspaper describing the accident. When I saw my name
printed there, I instantly felt myself to be carrying a public
branding, visible to all. Again the spinning, whirring sensation entered my head emphasizing still further the sensation
of occupying a different dimension of time and space from all
others. I struggled to remain conscious and then I struggled
to remain silent, unsure whether the scream that was inside
me was also being expressed outside.

I arrived at work in a daze but somehow managed to
function in a normal enough manner to get to my locker,
retrieve my headset and make my way to the exchange floor.

Upon starting one's shift, the first task was to clock on and then report to the monitor who would tell you your board number (different boards answered different calls, e.g., long-distance calls, complaints, directory inquires, general inquires etc.).

Alarm bells should have rung when I was placed on the 012 board. It was the board closest to the monitor's desk and it was the easiest of all the positions. Being assigned there usually meant that you were either the monitor's pet or you were in trouble for talking too much to other operators and were therefore being placed under the monitor's nose for some firm disciplining. I don't recall giving a second thought to my placement; I just sat down grateful to be back in safe, familiar territory. Needless to say, I wasn't exactly behaving in my usual manner. Normally I would have scanned the room to see where my friends were sitting, and at the first opportunity I would have broken the sacred rule of the exchange and phoned them for a gossipy chat. The monitors hated us phoning each other and were able to inflict serious consequences on people caught red-handed, but no matter, we all did it anyway and usually got away with it. Today I avoided looking for my friends; somehow I knew that they would be my undoing. But it took only a few minutes before the operator next to me whispered, 'Answer the next call, it's Eve.'

I knew that Eve was calling me to talk about the trip, which was now only three weeks away, and I could see from glancing towards her that she knew nothing about the horror of yesterday. I answered the call and listened silently while she exulted over something or other, then when she had finished I told her that I couldn't go on the trip because I had to go to court. When she asked why, I replied, 'Because I've killed somebody.' With those words, I fell apart and collapsed into a sobbing mess. The monitor, who had been on duty the previous day when the police phoned to explain my absence, was beside me in a flash and I realized that she had been waiting for something like this, hence my close proximity to her. She took me outside and beckoned Eve to follow. We all went upstairs to the sickroom where I continued to weep for quite some time. Eve was appointed as my companion and comforter but I suspect she was too shocked and baffled by this turn of events to have properly comprehended the task the monitor had thrust upon her.

After I had calmed a little, Eve and I were given permission to take the rest of the day off. I don't remember where we went or what we did, but by evening we were at Eve's house having a meal with her mother whom I hadn't previously met. In fact, I had never been to Eve's house before and was shocked to discover that she lived disturbingly close to the accident scene. During the evening the talk got around to discussing the possibility that I would be imprisoned for manslaughter. Eve made jokes about helping me break out, but the sickening whirring began again, reminding me that from now on I would always be condemned to stand apart, outside of, banished from, the normal things of life.

Eve's mother made up a spare bed for me and we all retired for the night. Why did I choose to stay there instead of going home? I do not remember. Did I inform my parents that I wasn't coming home? We didn't have a phone at home but it is possible that I had phoned my mother at work to tell her. Whatever my original reasons for staying there, I became uneasy while lying in the dark of Eve's house. I lay there for some time trying to work out what I should do. Should I wake Eve and tell her I was going? How would I get home? Why did I even want to go?

I didn't answer any of these questions but at some point I simply stopped asking them, got out of bed, dressed in the dark, and quietly slipped out of the house. I don't recall how I actually got home but I suspect I walked the 80-minute journey. When I arrived home it was the early hours of the morning; the house was quiet and dark, and everybody was in bed. My bedroom was a partitioned annexe off the back veranda, making it unnecessary for me to enter the house. I got into bed without anybody knowing I was there and cried myself into a lonely and exhausted sleep.

Next morning I discovered that my father had taken the previous day off work to wait at home in case I needed to leave work early. Nobody had bothered to tell me; the only reason I found out at all was due to overhearing my father jokingly telling my brother about the arrival of the accident investigators who had come to photograph the car. My father thought they were press photographers and ran out of the house to order them away. He then casually commented, 'Bren didn't come home, so I suppose she must have coped all right. I didn't need to take the day off after all.'

The sequence of events over the next few days is something of a blur. At home we continued to be polite but strained with each other, a situation exacerbated by the discovery that my mother had decided to go to the woman's funeral without taking me along or even discussing it with me. The question of attending the funeral had only occurred to me a week or so after the event. I asked my mother whether I should have gone, to which she immediately replied, No! As an after-thought, she then told me that she had gone in my place. I probably should have been grateful, but instead I was deva-stated. If she felt I needed to be represented then she should have spoken to me about it. I wanted to do the right thing but

I needed some guidance. I was completely out of my depth but we all just kept pretending that life was normal.

At work few people said anything directly to me but one morning while sitting at a table with five or six operators during a tea break, a young woman breathlessly asked the group whether we had heard that somebody in the exchange had killed a woman. 'Yes, it was me,' I replied. Then, as much out of embarrassment for her as for me, I left the table.

I asked to be rostered only afternoon shifts, 3 pm–11 pm, which allowed me to avoid seeing anybody at home by remaining in bed during the morning rush and by getting home after everybody else had retired. It also meant that I encountered fewer people at work. Sometimes I would still go out dancing after work with my friends, but apart from the temporary relief obtained by being in a dark, noisy environment where conversation was limited, there was little enjoyment to be had. Even Joe avoided talking to me; or perhaps it was I who avoided him.

Then, unexpectedly, my mother suggested that I should still go on my trip; she said that it was possible for me to request permission to leave the State while the Coroner's hearing was pending. So late one night after finishing work, my parents took me to the police station to sign a statutory declaration detailing my travel plans and requesting permission to leave the jurisdiction. A few days later, I was advised to attend a special sitting of the Coroner's Court to give evidence prior to departing.

I had never attended Court before, nor I think had my parents. Neither was there a plethora of TV courtroom dramas in the early '70s to educate the populace about legal matters. The thought of phoning Joe was shameful; hence I walked into the courtroom totally unaware of, and unprepared for, what was to come. My parents both came with me, but not a word passed between us about what was to happen.

The first shock occurred before we even entered the courtroom. The clerk asked me some details about how I had arrived at the Court and then proceeded to give me some money! I was dumbfounded, but thankfully my father intervened and explained that the Court paid the cost of transport to get you to the hearing. My head was starting to spin again as the foreignness of this world descended upon me.

We were ushered into a cold, dark, bleak room, or at least that is how it seemed to me. Only a few people were present: one of the police officers who attended the accident was there; a clerk; a Court attendant; and of course the Coroner. A few formal announcements were made in a language and tone that turned my blood icy. I was then called to take the stand, though at first didn't realize what that meant so the attendant beckoned me to rise and follow his mimed instructions. A Bible was then placed in my hands and the oath was read to me. Outwardly, all that would have been observable was a momentary hesitation before docilely repeating the oath, but inside me a war had erupted.

I had rejected God, the church, and the Bible at age twelve when I defiantly and jubilantly declared myself an atheist. I had recognized what I perceived as the empty truths and destructive teachings of the Church when, at a school assembly, a visiting Bishop had exhorted us to love Jesus more than we loved our parents. His instruction made me realize that Jesus was not, and never had been, a reality for me. He was merely a pathetic figure who ceaselessly hung from a pathetic cross: not the stuff of love, but rather the stuff of scorn to my adolescent mind. From that moment the Church and religion were anathema to me. And yet, as the oath issued smoothly from my mouth, I realized I was not so defiant as to challenge the presumption of the Church's authority at this most precarious moment of my life.

Perhaps it was the shock of saying the oath, or perhaps it was a self-defence mechanism, or perhaps it was just bloody-mindedness, but from that moment I was once again incapable of thinking through the consequences of my actions. The Coroner asked me to describe what had taken place on the morning of the accident and I heard myself reply that I had already told the police what had happened. The Coroner asked me again to give the details, and again I replied that I could add nothing to what I had previously said. 'Are you refusing to give evidence?' he asked. I looked at him across the dim expanse of the room and despite having no idea why, I said, 'Yes.' With that I was dismissed from the stand and the proceedings quickly came to a close.

I was stunned by what had taken place, as no doubt were my parents. We left in silence. Once out of the building, Dad suggested that we stop at a coffee shop we were passing. We went inside and ordered drinks — I had a hot chocolate and raisin toast — and it occurred to me that I could not recall a single other occasion when just the three of us had ever done anything similar. We spoke little and soon Mum excused herself, saying she had a lot of work to catch up on. Dad and I stayed a little longer, engaged in a bit of small talk, and then went our separate ways.

However, with the legal impediments out of the way, my day of departure for Queensland rapidly approached. Part of me was glad to be leaving the hothouse atmosphere of both home and work; but another part of me was bitter and resentful that I was being packed off out of the way. No doubt I had become very unpleasant to live with; at home I was brittle, withdrawn, angry and frightened. I wanted to be protected and comforted, but had begun to lash out at anyone who dared to offer sympathy. My thoughts were almost completely devoted to finding fault with myself so that I could provide an answer to the question that now stood before me at every waking moment: *'Do I have the right to continue living now that I have caused a death?'* To me, the answer was clearly no; I didn't have the right. This might seem at odds with the gesture of defiantly claiming my life back from the angels and demons, but it should be understood that my experience of these events was not as clearly defined and differentiated as it might appear on paper. I was living in a waking nightmare where, as in real dreams, life segued from scene to scene, and while each scene had its own logic and integrity, that logic didn't necessarily carry over into any of the other scenes.

Neither did knowing the answer to my question help me to know how to act upon the answer. Nor did I have the courage to face the consequences of the answer, so instead I searched around for evidence of my unworthiness, discovering in myself an ability to turn even the most generous of gestures into proof of my disgrace. One day I arrived home to find an elderly male stranger sitting in the lounge room talking to my parents. My mother was clearly flustered that I had unexpectedly appeared, but she had little choice other than to introduce me. The man was the brother of the woman whom I had killed. He gently told me he was very pleased to have unexpectedly met me because he wanted to be sure I knew that the surviving family held no grudges against me. He urged me to put the event behind me and get on with my life. However, he said there was one question he needed to ask me. He asked whether the police report was correct in stating that his sister was walking away from the church rather than towards it. My confirmation of this left him puzzled. 'That is most odd,' he said, 'normally she would be going into church at that time, not leaving.' There was a moment of awkward silence before he excused himself and left. I was deeply touched by his gesture and immensely grateful for it, yet the overriding impact was one of further alienation. Why had my parents not advised me he was coming? The obvious answer was shame. They were ashamed of me. And why not! I was utterly ashamed of myself too.

A mere three weeks had passed since the accident. Three weeks of adjusting my self-perception from that of a gregarious teenager with the world at her feet, to that of a shameful killer who had no moral right to remain alive. Three weeks of terrifying nightly excursions to spiritual realms; of appalling inner torments; and of sickening expectations of a prison sentence. A mere three weeks, and now it seemed surreal to be leaving Perth on the famed Indian-Pacific train, along with my friends Eve, Margaret, and Susie. Mum and Dad were at the station to see me off. Stephen and I seemed to have been on a collision course since the accident, which surprised and upset me. Despite our lifelong competitiveness with other, we had always been fairly close, though lately there was something hurtful creeping in. Shortly before our departure, Steve had invited Eve and me to join one of his regular weekend surfing trips to the south coast. He went with five or six of his mates, who were boys I had known since school, so it seemed a good way of spending time with Steve and his friends before leaving. Steve and I were close in age and had similar interests, apart from surfing, so we had managed to retain the childhood habit of accepting each other's friends as our own. Inviting the other along to wherever we were going was normal behaviour, or rather it was before the accident. I hated surfing and the whole culture associated with it, but I accepted this invitation as a mark that things were returning to normal. Unfortunately, I was very wrong.

We left late on Friday evening, seven or eight of us crowded into Steve's panel-van. I don't know whether they had been drinking before, but the beer cans were out as soon as we took off. The drive to the coast took around four hours and for the latter part of it the road was steep and winding. Needless to say, a great deal had been drunk by this time; none of it by me though, as beer held no appeal whatever. As the drive progressed and the intoxication increased, my anxiety reached panic levels.

It wasn't just our safety that concerned me; I was devastated to discover that Stephen was utterly oblivious to my distress. Surely he should know that dangerous driving was now anathema to me? Couldn't he see that his behaviour was mocking my pain? I now believe that he was probably well aware of his actions. You see, only a few days after this, by way of apology, he asked me to see a movie with him. I agreed without inquiring which movie it was, however on the way there he revealed that he had already seen this movie a week before. 'It's fantastic,' he said, 'you'll love it.' The movie was It's a Mad, Mad World. Much of the opening 20 minutes of the film is devoted to reckless driving and 'funny' car crashes. I left the cinema to vomit and didn't return. Stephen was really annoyed that I had walked out. He seemed to take it as some sort of personal insult.

So, given the circumstances, I doubt that he came to the train station to say farewell. However, much of my memory of the departure is eclipsed by a single event that seemed innocent enough at the time but which proved to be much more significant than I had realized. It involved my father

Frederick, my soul mate and ally within the family. Dad is the only member of the family I never remember arguing with. Mum would say that's because he was never around, or when he was home he was reading the paper or watching television. There is a certain truth in that, but only a partial one. My experience of Dad's company is quite different.

I adored my Dad and I'm completely confident that he adored me. He was typical of his generation in not showing his feelings openly or talking about deep and meaningful things, but he had a way of making gestures that expressed his intentions. For example, in the weeks between the accident and my departure, Dad would often come home to have lunch with me. It was always the same ritual; he would appear with a can of scotch broth soup and some crusty bread. He would prepare the meal, which we ate at the kitchen table while discussing current events from the newspaper, or exchanging light banter about work or home or friends. We never talked about the accident; it would have been too much for him to defy my mother's edict against mentioning it, but I knew that his presence was an attempt to offer some healing balm.

I had come to accept that Dad spoke in gestures not words and was therefore taken aback when he behaved completely out of character at the train station. I had said all my final goodbyes and was just about to step onto the carriage when Dad caught hold of me in a tight embrace. He told me that he loved me and that I should take care, but just as I was about to break free of his embrace, he tightened his hold and added some extra words that quite stunned me. He seemed distressed, which surprised me, I had not been expecting any display of emotion; we were a family who just did not do that!

I eventually broke away from his embrace and got onto the

train trying to look composed and normal. I joined my friends and pushed the discomforting moment away. I can no longer recall just what it was he said to me in those final moments; sometimes I think it was an apology for the accident, or even an apology for his life; or perhaps something quite different. Whatever it was, I regret that I did not listen more attentively to what turned out to be the last words he ever spoke to me.

4

June 1971–August 1973

The train journey took me once again across the vast Nulla-bor desert, and although none of my many subsequent crossings ever compared to the impact of the first, it was still an inspiring journey. The excitement of our adventure, coupled with the heady novelty of travelling on a train that inspired pride in the heart of most Australians, was suffi-ciently distracting to give me a short respite from my morbid moods and thoughts. The sleeping cabins were extra-ordinarily small, but so ingeniously designed as to be entrancing, holding some of the same fascination and ambi-ence as a doll's house. Everything was very practical, but somehow magical. My favourite design-feature was the way in which the corridor perpetually wound itself into a never ending S-shape as it bent and curved itself around the out-jutting cabins.

After a three-day journey we arrived in Melbourne for a two-week visit before heading up to Queensland. This was meant to be one long party to celebrate our new-found independence, our rite of passage as young women stepping out into the world. But my rites of passage were already well underway and they bore little comparison to the rituals my friends were eager to participate in now they were free of parental constraints and worries.

For me, the big questions of life did not include such issues as, who's the best looking boy in the room and is he looking at me? I too, it is true, derived a certain satisfaction from the simple adolescent ceremonies of wearing outrageous clothes and makeup and attending night-clubs and pubs (illegally, because we were under 21) without concern about curfews or what time we got home. Yet the stark difference between my reality and theirs was undeniable.

I was becoming ever more consumed by one essential question: *Do I have the right to continue living now that I have caused a death?* It was a sickeningly heavy burden to realize that nobody in my circle of friends or family could help me answer this question. It offered further proof that I was doomed to live a life apart. The only certainty the future held for me was that I would soon be in prison, serving my sentence for manslaughter. The prospect, though terrifying and repugnant, held a certain comfort; somehow it seemed preferable to be where my shame could be transparent, rather than continuing the deception of invisibility that 'normal' life allowed.

Nevertheless, despite my torments and morbidity, Melbourne was rather enjoyable. It is a much bigger city than Perth, so everything seemed a little more exciting and sophisticated, which encouraged us to believe that we also had taken on some of those qualities. We left Melbourne to hitchhike to the Gold Coast region of Queensland; this risky form of travel was intended to further confirm (to ourselves?) that we were independent beings who could fearlessly push barriers apart. Hitchhiking is meant to be somehow exciting, romantic even, and while this may be true, it is also a hard and fairly tedious form of travel. We set off in two groups, Eve and I, and Sue and Margaret. We were heading first for the Gold Coast, via Sydney, because we planned to spend another two weeks partying before leaving for our final destination of Green Island in far north Queensland. The journey from Melbourne to the Gold Coast covered some 2,000 kms, so we pre-arranged to meet each other at certain towns along the way to ensure each other's safety.

Only one incident occurred which could have been troublesome. Eve and I were travelling with a semi-trailer driver who was unusually quiet. We didn't really mind his quietness, it was a bit of a relief after having encountered several very talkative drivers, but we became nervous when he turned off the road onto a secluded lay-by. After the truck had stopped, he silently got out of his seat and clambered into the sleeping section at the rear of the cab. He reached under the bed and produced a collection of porn magazines that he proceeded to read while silently gesturing for Eve and me to join him. We quickly excused ourselves and ran to the road, nervously glancing backwards to check if he was following us. Fortunately he didn't, and we kept running until another lift came along, which thankfully wasn't long.

We arrived at the Gold Coast without further incident and found ourselves a holiday flat at Surfers Paradise. I had not been looking forward to another fortnight of partying, but to my surprise I immediately felt a strong sense of ease, comfort almost, in the surrounds of the Gold Coast. Why that might be is baffling. There is no doubt it is a gorgeous place, at least as far as the natural environment goes, but busy beach resorts are definitely not high on my 'desirable places to visit' list. And yet for me the stay was too short, I was overwhelmed by a great sense of loss and discomfort upon leaving. My discomfort continued to grow the further north we travelled, until, at Mackay, 1,500 kms north and half way to our final destination, I realized I had to turn around and return to Surfers Paradise.

My companions didn't take this revelation well, partly because they initially assumed I was demanding we all return to Surfers; then, when it became clear I was intent on going alone, they were concerned for my wellbeing. I couldn't explain my decision, either to them or to myself. It made no sense whatsoever, of that much I was well aware. Yet neither could I deny the maelstrom of chaos that was enveloping me with each step. I simply had to get back.

This sense of certainty in following an irrational decision is one that has continued to define and direct my life. Time and again I find myself compelled to swim against the tide, often exasperating and confusing those around me. However, this time, in deference to the concern of my friends I did make one concession, I agreed to catch the train back, rather than hitchhike alone.

Once on the train, I soon became aware of a group of three young men, a couple of years older than me. Before long they struck up a conversation and invited me to sit with them. They were travelling to Rockhampton, about 500kms south, to meet up with a team of young people who roamed the regional towns of Australia selling art prints to provincial folk. 'We'll only be there for two days,' they said, 'why not join us?' So, in the early hours of the morning, I disembarked from the train with my new-found friends. We slept on the station platform until dawn and then walked into town to find the home of the person overseeing the team.

The selling of the art prints didn't commence until early evening, which meant we had the rest of the day off, so we headed to the local pub. A lazy lunch in a regional pub with three young blokes would not normally be the setting for learning one of life's great lessons, but that day I learnt something for which I still remain grateful.

One of the three was a brash, confident type who dominated the conversation and called the shots; another was his
fall guy, setting up the gags and egging him on. These two
were so entertaining that I had hardly taken any notice of the
third, quieter member of the trio, who I will call Ryan. At
some point the noisy two departed, leaving Ryan and me
alone. I was on a high from the sheer relief of being with
people who knew nothing about my shameful past, and who
were engaging with life in an uncomplicated, ordinary way. I
had laughed more in the previous few hours than in the two
months since the accident. But what was I laughing about? As
it turns out, something very unfunny.

'Brash' had been making fun of the people in the pub, the
town, and the provincial nature of the surroundings. When
he left I attempted to carry on with the jokes, but they fell
absolutely flat on Ryan. With a start I realized that he hadn't
participated in the joke telling at all, in fact he was now
looking around at the people and surroundings with total
acceptance and genuine love. There was not a critical or
sarcastic element to him whatsoever, not even towards his
friends who were of quite the opposite temperament to
himself.

In that moment, I suddenly felt very conscious of the lessons I had been taught during the evening 'trials' with the
angels and demons. I reflected on my motives in finding
humour in belittling others, and conceded that my behaviour
was driven by the need to feel that others were less worthy.
Being in Ryan's presence changed my perspective and
shamed me to aspire to emulate his ability to be accepting of
all. I have yet to achieve that goal, but many times in my life
when I've strayed too far from it, I have been blessed by the
memory of this moment of awakening. I was blessed in other

ways also to have met this remarkable young man with whom I spent a total of three days.

The selling of the art prints involved being driven to the residential areas of the town, door-knocking the appointed homes, showing sample prints to the residents and, hopefully, taking their orders. I declined to do any selling, and instead was permitted to sit in the car with the team leader, observing the progress. It was only when the evening was over and we were being driven back to the team leader's home that I began to wonder about the sleeping arrangements.

We were given the floor of a rear, enclosed veranda as our sleeping space, and Brash immediately announced that I could share his sleeping bag. 'No need,' Ryan replied, 'I've already offered to lend her my sleeping bag.' It wasn't true of course, we hadn't discussed it at all, but I accepted his offer with enormous relief, and not a small amount of chagrin that I had completely failed to recognize the potential danger of the situation.

Next day we resumed our train journey to Brisbane. I was then catching a bus to Surfers, which as it turned out was the same bus that Ryan was catching to Sydney. Before boarding the bus we went to the Brisbane Post Office so that I could collect my mail. Among the letters was one from Mum that contained a newspaper clipping about the Coroner's verdict.

At first I just looked at it blankly, this was not the way I had expected to hear the outcome, nor was it the outcome I was expecting. The clipping reported that the Coroner had declared an Open Verdict. This meant there was insufficient evidence either to clear me or to formally charge me, which legally left the case open for a further seven years. Essentially, it left the decision in the hands of the police, giving them seven years to decide whether to proceed with charges. Emotionally, it left me in a precarious state of limbo.

I knew that all it would take for me to end up in prison was for someone to calculate my speed from the skid marks, or for a witness to confirm that the woman was on the crossing. Once that was done, the lie in my statement would be revealed and I would be behind bars, guilty of both manslaughter and perjury. However, until those calculations were done, or witnesses came forward, the Coroner's verdict left me with no choice other than to inflict my own punishment, which ultimately proved to be far more severe than any court in the land would have chosen.

I have no recollection of what I did upon arriving in Surfers. Somehow I ended up with a job and a room in a shared flat, but how that came about is completely lost to me. My job was as a Radio Operator for a local taxi firm, a small outfit whose office was located in the side office of a petrol station. I worked the afternoon shift, alone, from 3pm–11pm. The garage closed at 6pm, so for most of my shift I was the only person on the premises.

My accommodation, a sparse, cheap, two-bedroom flat, situated only a few minutes from both the beach and the main street of Surfers, was shared with three young men (and their assorted girlfriends) who ran a niche coffee shop in Surfers called My Place. It was a bohemian affair, open from 9pm to around 3am, serving mostly hot chocolate and raisin toast, and playing a lot of Cat Stevens tracks. It was a tiny, dark place, tucked into the corner of a plaza of shops; and for a while it was my refuge. I felt comfortable there because it was the one place where most of my peers were in a worse emotional state than I was.

Many people in the cafe used drugs. Marijuana, speed, and

acid were the norm, though heroin was not uncommon. Using them myself had no appeal whatsoever; I was already in an altered state of consciousness, and frankly found it unfathomable that anybody would willingly distort or risk a normal mind. Yet I was both comfortable with and comforted by the overt declaration my new-found friends were making about their own brokenness. They, in turn, seemed to find my straightness equally comforting; it meant there was someone in the house, in the cafe, who could be relied on. One of my flatmates even came to rely upon me to assist him in shooting heroin.

Perversely, it was not long before being considered reliable became an intolerable burden. How, I would ask myself, can a person who has killed, moreover a person who has got away with killing, be considered a good and reliable person? Particularly chilling was the prospect that my fraudulent reliability might contribute to a drug-related death. I started to ask myself whether I was fated to be some kind of serial killer. Perhaps it was a mistake to end the spiritual trials; what if my behaviour over the past weeks had tipped the balance in favour of the demons? What if their influence was now controlling me?

One night, in an attempt to prove my unworthiness, I ditched my straight image and dropped acid. It was horrible. I felt disassociated from my body, unable to control or influence my mind, and awash with alien feelings and images. The worst of these was a crushing fear of cars that paralyzed me. I couldn't cross the street, and I certainly couldn't bear the thought of actually getting into one of the things. They were abhorrent, fearful, evil. Where did those thoughts and feelings come from? Were they my true feelings or were they produced through distortion or trickery? I had no way of knowing; but I knew for certain that I would not find answers or solutions through drugs.

Shortly after this, my friends Eve, Margaret and Sue arrived back at Surfers. Things had not worked out on Green Island, so they cut their losses and headed back. It was great to see them again and we immediately set about finding a rental house to share. After we had moved in together it became apparent that their path of self-expression and independence was being explored through casual sex. Couplings would take place at all hours of the day and night, sometimes in the very bed I was sleeping in! We could only afford a small two-bedroom house, so Eve and I shared one double bed, and Sue and Marg the other. It was great for the rent, but caused severe disruption to my sleeping habits, particularly when I sought refuge on the couch only to find it was also in use.

In many ways I found this far more confronting than living with drug users. It forced me to address my own sexuality and all the related issues of trust, intimacy and self-image. They were places far too painful for me to go to. Instead I retreated into sullenness and criticism. It wasn't just the sex thing that unnerved me; my friends were hanging out with some unpleasant characters who liked to play games with Ouija boards. Normally I kept a low profile during these 'sessions' but one time the spirit announced itself as the Devil. It declared that it was too powerful to be contained in a glass and needed to speak through a person. It singled me out as the only suitable person in the room. I told everyone to get stuffed and stormed out of the room.

Where this kind of lifestyle might have led can only be speculated upon because before long a letter arrived from my mother telling me that she and Dad had separated and that she wanted me to come home. The news was a shock but not really a surprise. I just assumed this was a similar situation to the last separation; surely the same reconciliation would happen. But this time it was not to be.

The situation I returned to was very different from the one I had left. Shortly after my departure from Perth, my parents had bought a smaller, newly built two-bedroom unit on the other side of the city after selling the family house to my aunt Wynne, Mum's older sister. They had also sold the Toyota Crown, and bought a smaller, newer car. What the motives were behind the changes I can only speculate; they were not discussed with me, but I suspect they represented drastic measures to deny the accident and the impact it had had on all of us. I knew that Mum could more easily convince herself of her mantra that 'we have to move on from unpleasantness' if that was backed up by a literal move to the other side of the city. And I knew that Jayne wanted to change schools to escape the taunts she claims to have received about having a killer for a sister. And Dad, well he would have just wanted a quiet life.

So when Mum revealed that she and Jayne had moved back into the old house with her sister, Wynne, with whom she has an intense love-hate relationship, it was clear the separation situation was dire. Yet returning home again wasn't nearly as traumatic as might be imagined. In fact, it all went rather smoothly, probably because the dynamics and parameters of the household had shifted dramatically. Wynne was now the power-broker/benefactor, with Mum very dependent on her sister's goodwill. Jayne was distraught and rebellious over the marriage break-up and the return to old territory. Steve was once again absent; still on his extended working holiday around Europe and England. And I, well I was no longer viewed as potentially bringing further public shame on the family by being sent to prison. I suppose with hindsight, we were experiencing the calm of the eye of the storm.

The only difficulty occurred shortly after my return home when Dad called by to take Jayne on an outing. He seemed shocked when I opened the door, but did not say a word; perhaps he didn't know of my return. It was an awkward, poignant moment for both of us. My enduring memory is of a frozen fragment of time in which we both sat silently in the lounge room waiting for Jayne to come and break the tension. It was to be our last meeting ever. Soon after this, without saying a word to anybody, Dad left Perth. The first we knew of his departure was when informed by the police that he had abandoned the car outside the Adelaide offices of the company that had financed the car loan. Why he chose Adelaide was a mystery, but to me it made sense that he had chosen to drive across the Nullabor. Surely he was searching its vast expanses for the same answers I sought. He was haunted as keenly as I; the demons that spoke to him in the dark of the night held their own special terror that only he will ever know about.

Strange to say, in some ways Dad's departure had a positive, healing outcome for me. Since the accident I had become convinced that he was suffering tremendous pain and grief over what he perceived as his culpability in my guilt and shame. His dramatic vanishing gesture only served to confirm this conviction, which in turn alleviated some of my pain. It offered some validity to my own suffering, some proof that I wasn't completely alone in feeling wretched about having caused the violent death of another human being. The effect of this healing was to allow me six months of relative normality.

I successfully reapplied for my old job at the telephone

exchange, and surprisingly it was very reassuring to return there.

At work I renewed an acquaintance with a young woman of my age who would become one of my closest friends, Margaret Johnson. We had worked together previously, but shortly before the accident Margaret had left Perth to spend a few months in Melbourne. When we met up again, she wasted no time telling me that she knew what had happened and was concerned for my welfare; a gesture I found very touching given that it was so rare. We quickly discovered that we had a lot in common, including being born only a few days apart. We also shared a love of dancing and clubbing so before long we started visiting my old dancing haunts, and within a few weeks we arranged to share a flat together.

The flat was in Bay Apartments, a former nurse's residence in the city: it was sparse and drab, and it only had one bedroom but we had the best time living there.

We would work the afternoon shift, 3pm–11pm, then dance until 3am at the Waldorf club, which was only a short walk from our flat. The walk home involved passing the emergency entrance to Royal Perth Hospital, where less than a year before my nightmare had begun. Did it upset me to walk past there? No, mostly because we found a very good way of distracting ourselves from it. Opposite the hospital stood a large Cathedral that we had to pass by one of three ways. We could walk the path between the hospital and the Cathedral; we could walk through the Cathedral grounds; or we could walk around the far perimeter.

Every evening, during the three or four minute walk from the club to the Cathedral, we would speculate on what might be lying in wait for us by the darkened grounds. Sometimes, as we approached, we thought we saw movement on one side or other, so would dash to the other side clutching each other in thrilled fear. Other times, we marched up there defiantly, boldly walking through the gates, daring any ghoul, human or otherwise, to show its face! Mind you, it only took a gust of wind to set us running for our lives. But it served the good purpose of keeping me from dwelling on what had taken place just across the road in the emergency waiting room.

Working the evening shift certainly suited our lifestyle; and, because it paid higher rates, it also suited our budget. We soon felt so flush with money that we started wondering how we could spend it all. What could we do and where could we go that would be suitably exciting for two such sophisticates? Perth seemed terribly provincial to us now that we had both tasted the delights of travel, but returning to the 'eastern states' wasn't very appealing either. Nor did we want to go to England and Europe on the same old 'working holiday' that every other young Aussie (including Steve) was doing. No, we wanted something different, something that set us apart. Then, in a moment of mutual inspiration, we both exclaimed, 'Munich! Let's go to the Munich Olympics.'

Quite why the Olympics were so appealing I don't know; neither of us had the least interest in sport, but somehow the notion took hold. It was fantastically exciting to plan and prepare for our trip; and, as expected, lots of people were suitably impressed by our choice.

Life was becoming sweet again, and I had a good friend with whom to share plans and goals for the future. Through this my sense of self, my sense of social norms, and my sense of where I fit within society began to come back into focus. Before the accident, these things were not an issue; I was just me, part of the mass, largely indistinguishable from the rest (though desperate to be different). After the accident, I was no longer me; I ceased to exist, society had banished me, the shrouded world of the dead had claimed me. Could I now hope to return to a normal life? Could I finally give an affirmative answer to the relentless question that still lingered: *Am I worthy to be part of society again?*

How I would have dealt with this question amidst the terrible tragedy of the Munich Olympics thankfully did not arise. We changed our minds about going to Munich on a sudden whim. The day we were due to pay for our tickets, we dropped our guard and went looking at the new winter fashions that had just been released.

Our undoing was the collection from the hot young designers of the day, Mr John and Merivale. The clothes were so stunning that we immediately opted to spend our savings on a new wardrobe. My main purchases were: a black leather jacket, mid thigh length, with a front zip and wide buckled belt; a blue leather jerkin that zipped up the front and could either be worn as a mini dress or as a sleeveless jacket; and a pair of knee-high, blue suede platform boots. With the remainder of the money we decided to head for the only bright lights we could still afford; a working holiday in Sydney. I felt fantastic; it was almost possible to believe that the worst was over.

The move to Sydney went well initially; or at least I assume it did. Much of my memory of this time is fragmentary. I can only recall isolated incidents – the lines that join their dots are missing or unavailable to me at present. I recall the flat where Margaret and I lived in North Sydney, and I recall frequently encountering political propaganda about the historic 1972 election and Gough Whitlam's 'It's Time' campaign for the Australian Labor Party. I remember watching the news reports about Whitlam's sweeping victory, but then the image suddenly shifts to me sharing a different Sydney flat with my mother and Jayne. I don't know why they came to Sydney, I don't know what happened in between, and I don't know what happened to Margaret.

My next clear memory is of walking through a park off Broadway, near the city centre, lying down in the sun and falling asleep on the grass. Some time later two young policemen, who were concerned for my welfare, woke me. I assured them that I was all right, but they wanted my name and phone number as a precaution. After giving them my details I went home and met up with Kelly, the young girl who lived in the flat downstairs with her Mum. She was around four years old and liked me to take her to play on the swings in a nearby park. This time, as we played, she insisted that we swap names; I had to be Kelly, and she became Bren. It had never occurred to me to change my name but in that instant I knew I had been given my solution. I would simply do away with Bren and become Kelly; a new person with no history, no problems, no fears, no doubts, and no haunting questions.

When I got back home, the phone was ringing; it was one of the young policemen asking me out on a date. I said no, but I knew he was going to be persistent. He said he was worried about me and I needed someone to look out for me. His accuracy was terrifying. It was exactly what I needed, but perversely I couldn't bear knowing that my need was now becoming obvious to total strangers. He was all the proof I needed that it was time to split and start afresh. I packed a bag and left immediately.

My next image is of staying in a room at the People's Palace, a large establishment run by The Salvation Army, near Sydney's Central Station, which was an early precursor of YHA and backpacker-type places, except it was home to misfits more than travellers. I had first stayed there with my travelling companions when we were hitching from Melbourne to Surfers the year before. We chose it partly because it was much cheaper than anywhere else, and partly for the thrill of staying somewhere so wickedly decadent. Having homeless drunks and bag ladies as our fellow occupants was curiously satisfying, allowing us to be in close proximity to life's unfortunates, while knowing we were a class apart. This time, though, no such distinction protected me. I was not only physically homeless and very broke; I was also adrift without the anchors of family or identity.

My first priority was to get a job, but first I had to pawn my watch to get enough cash to pay for a week's accommodation and a few days' food. Then, while walking through the city centre trying to figure out how to compose a relevant work history for Kelly, I saw a notice advertising a vacancy at Cue, a very trendy clothes boutique in Regents Arcade. Without thinking twice, I went into the store and applied for the position. The manager's selection criterion was a simple one, anybody who looked the part was asked to spend two hours in the shop on trial. Then, whichever candidate sold the most merchandise got the job. It was my good fortune to be the last candidate he was trying out, and by a sheer fluke (a customer came back to purchase an expensive item she'd tried on earlier in the week), to get the best sales figures. So, at the end of my trial he offered me the position, starting immediately. It was just the sign I needed to confirm that my decision had been right. Kelly was going to have a charmed life.

It was a bit weird working in a hip boutique by day then returning to the People's Palace by night, but so long as none of my colleagues found out why should it matter? At least, that's the logic I started with, and for a short while it held me together. When my first paycheque arrived there were so many sensible and necessary ways to spend it that only one decision was possible – blowing it on getting my hair shorn like Mia Farrow's. Kelly needed a new look to match her new life and something as radical and defiant as a near baldhead was just perfect.

My new look was such a success that I needed to show it off. So that night I visited a nightclub situated near the Palace. It was so wonderful to be back in the heat, smoke, sweat and noise of a club that I sought out the manager to ask if any jobs were available. His only reply was, 'Can you start now?'

Being a waitress in a club wasn't the same as being a customer; regrets about taking the job arose almost straight away, nevertheless I quit the boutique job (by way of no longer turning up) and ignored the clanging warning bells. It went alright for a week or so but then quickly came to an unhappy end one evening when I went to the club on a night off. While chatting with some of the regulars, one of whom was a close friend of the manager, they invited me to join them for a late supper. I didn't hesitate in saying yes, even though it meant being alone with 5–6 males. It wasn't unusual for me to be the sole female in a group of men and previously there had never been any cause for concern. Neither was I concerned this time when one of the men said he had to drop into his nearby bedsit to collect something.

It was a tiny room, much like a budget hotel room, consisting just of a minimal galley kitchen at the entrance, which opened onto a bedroom that had a built-in wardrobe with a double bed and small ensuite bathroom. I still wasn't concerned when we all crowded into the meagre space between the walls and the bed; but when somebody pushed me onto the bed and shouted, 'Get undressed, bitch!' I knew this was trouble. At first, I just laughed and started to climb off the bed, but I was savagely pushed back and somebody began pulling at my clothes, ripping off my jeans.

I should have been terrified, and on some level certainly was, but out of nowhere I was also erupting with fury. I pushed my attacker away and managed to rise to a sitting position. I sought out the eyes of the manager's friend and fixed a stare on him, shouting, 'How dare you do this to me, I trusted you!' He cast his eyes downwards, slumped to sitting position on the low cupboards that lined one wall of the room, and turned his head away. His posture told me it was a winning strategy, so one by one I scanned the room, held their eyes, and defiantly shouted my accusation. It worked; with eyes averted and shoulders sagged, they threw my jeans and my handbag at me and told me to get out.

As I left, the manager's friend followed me, apologising profusely and declaring that it really was only meant as a joke. His words didn't console me at all; if anything they confirmed the whole thing had been discussed beforehand. By now my righteous anger had worn off and I was beginning to shake uncontrollably from the dawning realization of what might have happened. I reached into my bag to find some comforting chocolate only to discover that my purse was missing. 'They took my purse,' I wailed, and with that I came completely undone, sobbing and shaking incessantly. That purse contained all the money I possessed in the world, which was precious little. The loss of the money was bad enough, but the theft of my purse left me with no doubt whatever of the malicious, premeditated intent of my attackers.

When we got back to the club, the manager's friend sat me

at the bar, bought me a drink, and then vanished. I don't know how long I sat there, still crying, before a young man whom I'd never seen before approached me and asked if he could help. I don't remember what I said or how the conversation progressed, but he offered to take me home and look after me for the rest of the evening. Reckless as it might seem, I said yes.

He was a stranger, a male stranger, yet despite what happened earlier, some part of me knew he could be trusted. Perhaps it was also a case of needing to prove to myself that some men, one man at least, was trustworthy. 'I'll look after you,' he said. And look after me he did. There was only one bed in his flat, which we shared, but he didn't touch me. Next morning he got up and went to work, telling me to help myself to breakfast. He left money on the table for bus fares, but told me I could stay in the flat for as long as I wanted to. The idea of remaining was briefly tempting, but I was gone within an hour of his departure.

I had to find a new job. There was no way I was going to return to the club and serve drinks to any of the would-be rapists, but I needed money quickly as the rent on my room at the Palace was due. Despair was sweeping over me when I glanced across Pitt Street and saw a billboard for an employment agency that specialized in live-in jobs. I went straight in.

The agency placed me immediately as housekeeper for a family in the exclusive suburb of Double Bay. The wife was a self-employed pharmacist, the husband an academic, and the two kids were in primary school. It was awful. The family themselves were pleasant enough, but I couldn't bear being back in a domestic setting. It was particularly disturbing to be around intelligent, articulate people who wanted to engage me in conversation. For the first time I had to confront the immense difficulty of providing a plausible, coherent life history for Kelly Connor. I also had to recognize that Bren Connor wasn't going to be so easy to discard. She kept demanding acknowledgement, but the pain of revealing her was now too excruciating.

I lasted just three days before ringing the agency and begging for another placement. They moved me to a housemaid's position in a largish boarding house. That was better because I didn't have to talk with anyone; I just vacuumed the floors and cleaned the bathrooms, then retreated to the privacy of my cell. I didn't know it, but I was starting to go mad. It was clear enough that something was wrong but a visit to the local GP only compounded the problem. He diagnosed thrush and glandular fever, which to his mind indicated an active sexual life.* He gave me some 'nudge, nudge, wink, wink' advice about taking things easy, then sent me on my way. Needless to say, after the near-rape his response was devastating.

Two other major destabilizing factors were also in play; I was completely socially isolated, and my name change left me in a state of increasing uncertainty about who I was. Calling myself Kelly gave me a certain amount of relief from the burdens that Bren carried, but it also removed the last foundation of my identity. I now had no family, no home, no friends, and no history. At first it was fun and invigorating to be free to make up anything I wanted about myself, but it

---

* It's a relief to note that Louise Hay's *Heal Your Body* (Hay House, 2003) has a more relevant and accurate understanding of these diseases. She describes the cause of thrush as, 'Anger over making the *wrong* decisions.' And glandular fever as, 'Anger at not receiving love and appreciation. No longer caring for the self.' How very apt.

became an increasingly hollow and futile exercise. The meaninglessness of it overwhelmed me. I was desperately lonely but couldn't reach out to anyone. Kelly didn't *have* anyone to reach out to; and as for Bren, well Dad was the only member of my family with whom I still felt some degree of empathy, and he had vanished into oblivion, abandoning me to deal alone with a horrible fate that we should have been carrying together.

Estrangement between Mum and me was no real surprise; we had been warring with each other from the beginning. Our first 'battle of wills' was a commonly told piece of family folklore involving my unplanned and untimely conception, and my even more untimely birth. The story goes that my mother awoke early one morning, around 5am, with early labour pains. As this was her second child she was confident that the birth would take place later in the day, so went back to sleep. (Home-birth was the common practice in England during the 1950s with the local midwife on call for the birth.)

However, Mum awoke again less than two hours later and realized that my birth was imminent. She woke Dad and told him he would have to deliver the baby. 'Not likely!' was his response as he scrambled to get dressed and out of the house to get the midwife who lived close by. When they returned, Mum was pressing her hands against my relentlessly emerging head, trying to prevent the inevitable. The midwife only managed to get one arm out of her coat before I pushed my way into the world. Mum would often finish telling this story with the following refrain, 'And she is still too pushy and headstrong!' Yet, to give her due credit, she also frequently said that my birth had turned around the family fortunes. My father found permanent employment as a bus driver, and the Manchester Housing Council upgraded our accommodation from a small flat to a three-bedroom house on a new housing estate.

Strange to say, in retrospect it seems that the accident caused us all to fall into a replication of the birth experience. I was trying to push my way into an understanding of another world, another dimension of life, while Mum defiantly wanted to hold me back. Dad had again bolted though this time he wasn't about to burst through the door with a midwife.

I couldn't follow Mum's lead of denying the enormity of what happened, nor of what I'd experienced subsequently. She was equally unable to comprehend either my immersion in the process or my need to confront it. My situation became increasingly desperate; in part, my awareness of that desperation was emphasized by the wretchedness of people in the boarding house. All of them lived alone, many of them were lonely, and some were a bit deranged. One day, after vacuuming the room of a retired headmistress who had a germ phobia that required me to walk on tissues while vacuuming, I became frightened that I was heading in the same direction. Not knowing what else to do, I rang Lifeline and unburdened myself to a woman counsellor. Her response was to advise me to go to the nearest church, kneel before the altar, and ask for God's forgiveness and help. I slammed the phone down and wept angry tears of frustration and defeat.

The counsellor's advice was distressing on a number of levels. It plunged me further into isolation by confirming my estrangement from society, and it replicated the persistent refusal of people to allow me to talk about the pain. Perhaps most perilously though, it reminded me that I had experienced an aspect of the spiritual world which I couldn't trust sharing with anybody, not even a priest — perhaps most especially not with a priest.

From this moment, my memory shifts to walking alone through the streets of North Sydney, late at night. Was it the same day as calling the counsellor? I have no idea. I walked endlessly because I was frightened of what might happen if I stopped to face the reality that there was nowhere to go to, no one to go to. My wanderings were utterly aimless, yet almost at the point of exhaustion I found myself standing outside the casualty department of the Royal North Shore Hospital and suddenly I knew that this was where help could be found. A psychiatrist would listen to me. That was their job, wasn't it? I could tell everything to psychiatrists; they wouldn't be superstitious about spiritual matters, they wouldn't tell me not to talk about the pain, the guilt, or the shame. They would know about these things, they would help me.

I told my story of woe to the casualty doctor who arranged for me to see the consultant psychiatrist first thing next morning. It was the first ray of light to pierce my dark tunnel. Why hadn't I thought of this before? Next morning, I didn't hold back. The psychiatrist was younger than I expected, early thirties, dark hair and beard, small stature, rounding belly, smoking a pipe. Dr P. listened to me attentively but didn't say much, which I took as a cue to keep talking. After an hour's interview he quietly but firmly made the suggestion that I immediately admit myself for treatment. I didn't hesitate. I returned to my cell at the boarding house, collected my meagre belongings, got back to the hospital as quickly as possible and eagerly admitted myself to the psychiatric ward.

I was jumping from the frying pan into the fire.

5

August–October 1973

The psychiatric ward at the Royal North Shore Hospital is situated in a round, three-story building, adjacent to the main hospital. Its centrepiece, both architecturally and therapeutically, is a fabulous atrium filled with greenery. The ground floor consists of reception, consulting rooms, and the dining room. Upstairs are the wards, females on one side, males on the other, and below ground floor are therapy rooms, recreation rooms, and the laundry. Some patients didn't like the roundness; they felt mocked about being 'round the twist', but I remember the building with great affection.

The daily therapy routine began with a morning group therapy session for all residents and some outpatients. In the afternoon, a smaller, more intensive group therapy took place for a select group, which also included one or two out-patients. Individual consultations were rare; aggressive therapy such as electro-convulsive treatment was extremely uncommon. Chemical therapy was fairly standard, although it wasn't prescribed for me.

When not in therapy, the majority of our time was taken up with eating. Three meals a day, plus morning tea, afternoon tea, and supper, is a time-consuming business when eaten communally. The ward had its own kitchen, which not only provided good meals, but it also meant that food was pretty much always available. Mealtimes might not be considered official therapy, but they were certainly highly therapeutic. I found it incredibly comforting and encouraging to be amongst people who were living on the edge – living raw, living defiantly, living against the odds, living hopefully.

I opted to keep using the name Kelly because despite the grief it was causing me, I liked the name and felt a strong empathy with it. The consultant, Dr P., didn't particularly agree with my choice, but didn't strongly dispute it either. Part of my reason for keeping it lay in an incident that occurred several years before when I was about 15. My sister Jayne had innocently (or not) asked Dad what his favourite girl's name was. He pretended to think about it, but I smirked inwardly, knowing exactly what his answer would be, after all he had named me. Mum had named Steve and Jayne, but Dad had chosen my name above all others. It was part of our special connection.

Knowing that Dad liked my name was the only thing that made it bearable. It was a burden being called Brenda; Bren was just tolerable, but Brenda was so drab. Imagine, then, my shock when a name other than Brenda was Dad's answer. (I don't remember the name he said, but suspect it belonged to a popular actress.) I railed against him, demanding to know why he had lumbered me with such a dull name if it wasn't even his favourite! It's only now, as I write, that it occurs to me he might have just picked a neutral name to avoid a flare-up of sibling rivalry. Such is life.

My admission to the ward happened on a Friday afternoon, which meant I had a fairly low-key introduction to the life there. On Monday morning my first appointment was with the medical doctor for a physical check-up. He was youngish and seemed to present an odd mixture of bravado and nervousness; it occurred to me that he might not be very comfortable dealing with psychiatric patients, or perhaps just not with young women. It took all of five minutes before he blurted out his contempt for my short hair. 'Why do you want to cut your hair like a boy's?' he asked. 'You won't get any boyfriends looking like that, you know!'

'Good, don't want one,' I replied.

After another couple of days of assessment it was decided to include me in the small group therapy session. There were about seven in the group, including Dr P. We were not introduced to each other, so I had no idea of the issues and background of the others and they had none about mine. However, one of the participants was a woman in her 30s, an outpatient, who was clearly suffering from extreme anxiety. I don't know how long she had been in the group, but she was given considerable space to express a mixture of fear, anger, resentment and loathing towards the driver who had hit her as she attempted to use a pedestrian crossing. She wailed on and on about what a devastating effect this had had on her life and her family, and how wicked it was that the driver had got away without injury or consequence.

As I listened to her story my hands clenched into fists and I could feel my long nails piercing the skin of my palms. When asked by Dr P. how I was feeling, I revealed the blood in my hands and unleashed a torrent of fury towards the hapless woman. 'You selfish bitch,' I snarled, 'how can you possibly believe that the driver has suffered no injury. Don't you realize that your presence on the crossing has probably destroyed that man! You're the one who should be begging his for-giveness, you stupid cow!' I was as surprised as anyone else at the words that issued from my mouth, the feelings expressed were not part of my normal consciousness, and yet I was aware of feeling enormously relieved at having uttered them.

The session ended quickly after that and I went upstairs for a cup of tea to calm myself. A nurse soon joined me, and before long the drama of the afternoon was forgotten, at least by me, but not, I was to learn, by others. The afternoon passed quickly and preparations for the evening meal were underway. I excused myself to go to the toilet and thought nothing of it when the nurse accompanied me, although it did seem very strange when she didn't actually use the toilet herself, but just stood outside the cubicle and waited for me. She then followed me to the ward where my bed was situated, waited while I fussed around with some things, and seemed eager to join me when I went to sit in the atrium. Before long another nurse joined us, introduced herself to me as the evening staff, and cheerily bade farewell to the first nurse who was going off duty.

I was very touched by this show of conscientiousness to the new patient; my sense of being in the right place grew by the minute. We went into the dining room where the nurse stood beside me in the queue, then sat next to me at the table. We chatted amiably with the others at our table and I marvelled at my good fortune. At one point I again excused myself to go the toilet, and again the nurse rose to follow me. 'It's all right,' I called out brightly, 'I know the way.' There was a moment of silent tension before one of the women at the table laughed raucously and called out, 'Darlin', haven't you figured it out yet, you're on report, she *has* to go with you!'

She pointed to a large black diary that was kept in the dining room and gestured to me to go over and read it. Inside were comments from Dr P. about my dangerous display of aggression earlier in the day. It concluded with a directive that I was to be placed under 24 hours of close supervision to determine whether I needed to be moved to a more suitable venue (i.e. North Ryde Mental Hospital). I didn't know whether to be angry or proud when the woman placed her arms around my shoulders and congratulated me for being 'on report' from my first session.

The nurses apparently didn't find me 'dangerous' because I wasn't transferred to Ryde, but my 'aggressive display' led the consultant to make a decision that would ultimately have a very dangerous outcome for me. He called me to his office to inform me of the path my future therapy would take. He felt that the resolution of my 'agitation' lay not in exploring the circumstances and aftermath of the accident, but rather in identifying the deficiencies in my character that prevented me from dealing with the accident.

His theory was that my agitated mental state was not brought about by the act of having killed somebody, but rather, that the act of killing somebody had exposed a mental deficiency, i.e. an inability to adapt to a changed situation. He was convinced that my upbringing was at fault, that something had gone amiss in my early years which, once identified and treated, would allow me to live my life as if killing somebody were of no more importance than bumping into somebody in a crowd.

I was appalled by his attitude. I wasn't looking for a panacea to make the pain go away. I was asking for help to understand how I could carry this enormous burden through life. I didn't want to pretend that it hadn't happened. I didn't want to become blasé about death or the taking of life. I wanted to find a way to accept and carry the burden, without being crushed by it. Yet disagreeing with him would clearly have been counter-productive, I either would have been immediately transferred or discharged. Neither option was acceptable to me so I reverted to the game we played at home.

I kept (relatively) quiet and tried to do things his way, but inside the torment and destructiveness returned. It was destined to go on unabated, and, it seems, unnoticed, to its inevitable end.

I continued to attend both the morning and afternoon group therapy sessions, but as I couldn't mention the issue that was most important to me, they held little interest and had little positive outcome. With hindsight, the opportunity to explore some family history would and could have been a positive thing, as without doubt we all have dysfunctional aspects which need addressing. But the consultant chose the wrong time, place, and manner of addressing those issues. My mind was completely fixated on being a killer and on finding answers to the questions that mercilessly pursued me: *Am I worthy to go on living? Must I offer some recompense for the lost life? Is the 'trial' still going on without my knowledge? Is my soul in the hands of the angels or the demons? Why am I not in prison? When will the police recognize their mistake and come for me?*

The grave nature of these questions so utterly consumed me that nothing else mattered. My family, I'm sorry to say, were almost an irrelevance. Any capacity I might have had, or should have had, to feel concerned about working through my issues with them, had been all but eroded. They had clearly, undeniably, proven their unwillingness and/or inability to acknowledge my pain or assist in my recovery. Tragic though that was, it also seemed exquisitely appropriate. After all, I was a killer and therefore deserved all the pain I got.

On the ward a young woman patient in her mid-20s soon befriended me. She was a nursing sister who was admitted in an attempt to identify why she would cough and vomit blood whenever her marriage date was imminent. She was very kind to me and sometimes offered to take me home with her at the weekends. Almost all the residents went home at weekends, except me who had no home to go to. I quite liked having the ward to myself at weekends, it provided opportunities to have relaxed conversations with the nurses, and gave me time out to listen to music, read, or just sleep the day away. In other words, to be a normal adolescent for a change. After all, I was still only 19.

Life on the ward took a new turn when two other adolescents joined us. Martin, a 14-year-old schoolboy, was admitted after attempting suicide, whereas, Annie, a 19-year-old from a prominent Jewish family, was admitted to hush up a heroin addiction. The three of us quickly became firm friends, and boy! did it cause some jitters amongst the staff. Annie took me home with her one weekend and showed me where she kept her stash of heroin. She was still using regularly, but nobody at home or at the ward seemed to realize. While she was shooting up, Annie explained to me the importance of clearing air bubbles out of the syringe and described the horrible death that would result from air travelling through the veins. I listened with morbid fascination, aware that a terrible scenario was forming in my mind.

Young Martin also had a profoundly morbid effect on me. He never spoke about the reasons for his suicide attempt, nor did he express or display any suicidal tendencies, but just knowing he had made that choice fascinated me. He looked very elfin like, much like a younger version of the pop star Leo Sayer, and although he had a quiet demeanour, he was also very engaging. It was hard to reconcile oneself to the prospect of this lad finding life intolerable, which in turn caused me to take a more serious look at the option of suicide. Perhaps it might, after all, be the answer to my questions.

Yet life on the ward wasn't all gloom and doom; sometimes it was quite fun. My friends and I delighted in sending up one of the more ridiculous traditions of the ward; junior doctors carrying clipboards with questionnaires full of inane, stupid questions. The doctors were either so piously superior or so desperately nervous that it was usually impossible to resist giving them answers that you knew were going to upset them.

On one such occasion, the junior doctor who was luckless enough to have been assigned to me was somebody I had known prior to being a patient. Well, I didn't exactly know him, but our paths used to cross regularly. He would mow the lawns at the block of flats where I lived with Margaret Johnson. He would turn up every two weeks with his clapped-out old mower while his Dad, the owner of the flats, followed him around complaining about the poor job he was doing. My friend and I delighted in walking past during these tender father and son moments, because his face would always turn a brilliant scarlet colour. We knew that we were rubbing salt into his wounds, but the conventions of gender ritual demanded that we do it! After all, it's not often a girl gets to see a full-blown blush on a bloke...

Anyway, there we were sitting with the ubiquitous clipboard between us, neither of us offering acknowledgement of our mutual recognition, but recognizing each other nevertheless. The silly questions began, and I must say, he was far more professional and dignified than I imagined he could have been. But then, quite unexpectedly, the familiar scarlet shade appeared over his face. The next question had completely unnerved him; it was, 'Have you experienced an orgasm?...' My truthful answer was, 'I'm not sure, you'll need to describe one to me.' He didn't. Instead he clenched his teeth, set his jaw, ticked yes to the answer, and abruptly left.

Time slipped by quickly and soon enough it became apparent that decisions were going to have to be made about my future. A month was the usual maximum stay, and I was close to exceeding that. The thought of returning to the 'outside' world filled me with dread, but I put on a brave face and made some tentative steps. My first attempt at outreach was to make contact with my friend, Margaret Johnson. I've no memory of how I actually managed to locate her – through a mutual contact presumably – but somehow a message was given to her and she came to the ward to see me.

At the time, I had little appreciation of the courage it must have taken for her to come to the 'roundhouse', and I paid too little attention to her nervousness. It was a brief visit but I was thrilled to see her and began to feel the first surges of optimism about resuming a normal life. It was short-lived. Margaret's employer phoned the ward to say that she wouldn't be coming again. The family who employed her as a live-in nanny had advised her that it was dangerous to associate with me; they wouldn't tolerate her continuing to visit. I was devastated. The cracks that had been papered over suddenly shifted apart.

Next morning in the large group therapy, we played a game. Games weren't unusual in therapy and though I always participated, I kept myself aloof and immune to any outcomes. In this game, a collection of coins passed around the circle and each participant was required to select one. We then had to describe the emblem on the back of the coin and say why it had significance for us. My coin was the 10 cent piece, which I had selected without any interest or intent; but when it came to my turn to speak, I found myself devoid of any smart or deceptive comments.

Instead, the beautiful lyrebird looked up at me from behind its shield of feathers and I heard myself describing the distress of this reclusive bird that just wants to be left alone in the bush. But it suffers from the burden of being beautifully attractive; hence people seek it out to gawk at its beauty, intruding upon its reclusive nature.

If I had left my comments there, the situation might have been recoverable, but to my amazement I wasn't finished. When one of the nurses asked, 'What's the purpose of this paradox? Why does a creature that seems reclusive by nature have an attribute which draws attention to itself?' I should have shrugged my shoulders and kept my mouth shut. Instead, my eyes filled with tears and I wailed out, 'Because nobody really wants to be left alone.'

With that, all the grief, loneliness, rejection, fear, and heartache of the past two years burst forth. I sobbed through the remainder of the session, and when everyone left for lunch I remained in my seat, crying. I was still there when the afternoon group started and I cried through that as well. My distress seemed endless; eventually I was taken to bed, where I stayed until the next morning, probably sedated.

Common wisdom has it that crying is good for you, but that wasn't my experience. On awakening the next morning I was overwhelmed with wretchedness; I wanted to die, I wanted the misery to end. My resolve was clear. I walked out of the ward, went to a nearby pharmacy, bought some over-the-counter sleeping pills, walked to a small memorial park near the hospital, and swallowed all the tablets. Within a few moments, panic swept over me and I ran back to the ward to tell them of my mistake. A nurse took me to casualty where I was given a dose of Ipecac to induce a spasm of ghastly vomiting. Shortly afterwards, I returned to the ward, chastened and subdued and, once again, on report.

Something about this episode awakened a desire in me to contact my mother. Whether it was suggested to me, or arose spontaneously, I don't know. I only recall writing her a letter, explaining where I was, and asking for her help. She was again living in Perth with her sister Wynne, but upon receiving my letter she immediately resigned her job and came to Sydney with Jayne. They were given a small hospital flat reserved for emergency family use. It meant she was pretty much always by my side. It was a major mistake.

Our first joint session with the consultant was a disaster; we had a blazing row. I don't remember the details but they involved some perception on my part that Mum and Dr P. were colluding in diminishing the impact of the accident. The details were probably irrelevant because I suspect I would have taken any opportunity to release some of the fury that lived inside me. I stormed out of the office and, just before I banged the door shut, heard Dr P. call out that I was again on report. My heart froze; three reports guaranteed a transfer to Ryde.

I fled downstairs to the therapy room to hide before he could tell the nurses about the report. It was late afternoon so I knew that no one would be using the room, and I also knew that it was the last place anybody would look for me. Of all the rooms in the place, it was the one that nobody ever entered willingly. I wedged myself into a corner behind the chairs and considered my options. Going to Ryde was simply not on. I didn't know what went on there, but it was clear from the comments of the nurses that it was a place to be avoided.

The outside world gave no comfort or hope. Going home

with Mum was impossible; she had absolutely no intention of acknowledging the desperate pain I was in, or of providing the help and support that I needed and wanted. She was utterly stuck in her belief that denial provided the only solution. Dad offered no solutions. He was still playing his invisible man game. Stephen might have been able to help but he was in Europe. Margaret Johnson was the only friend who ever came close to offering support, and now she feared I was dangerous. And I had proven myself too cowardly to take the suicide option. What was I to do?

All I really needed and wanted was for someone to let me talk about my pain and my fears so that I could find a solution to the questions that preyed on me. I needed someone to give me permission to feel guilt for a horrible error of judgement that had resulted in a violent death. I needed assurance that I wasn't alone in believing that it's wrong to kill.

Then, in a moment of absolute clarity, I *knew* whom I needed to speak to: Margaret Healy, the woman I had killed. It was the perfect solution. Not only would I be talking to someone who intimately knew my guilt, but, by departing this world to enter hers, I would also be answering the questions that plagued me. It was now perfectly obvious I wasn't worthy to go on living. Some form of recompense had to be made for the lost life. Giving up my life was the recompense. I would give my life to Margaret Healy so that she could do with me as she pleased. But first, I had to make peace with those I would be leaving behind. I had to leave this world in such a way that nobody would ever know or guess my motives or my destination.

I emerged from the therapy room feeling calm, serene and utterly certain about my decision, but I entered a swirling maelstrom of chaos and anger. I had been missing for several hours, it was now mid-evening, and it seems my dis-appearance had caused some problems. In an attempt to locate me, the nurses and Dr P. had questioned Martin and Annie about where I might go and what I might do. They had cracked under pressure and revealed a conversation we had had some time before.

The three of us often went to the graveyard adjacent to the hospital. It's one of Sydney's oldest cemeteries, and at one time it would have been an elegant place to be laid to rest, but Sydney in the early 70s had not yet caught the heritage bug so the cemetery lay forgotten and largely neglected. Yet it was this very neglect that we found so compelling. To sit amongst the relics, to read the inscriptions on the headstones and tombs, provided some comfort in knowing that all things pass.

It was while being comforted by this thought, amongst the tombstones, that I had confided my secret to Martin and Annie. I described how I had stolen a hypodermic needle from the nurse's station, which I was keeping hidden for the day when I wanted to end it all. In ghoulish detail I expressed my expectation of the pain I would suffer as the air bubble coursed through my veins on its way to my heart. I thanked Annie for giving me the idea of the needle, and Martin for making suicide acceptable, and I thanked all the dead in the cemetery for giving me the perfect place to die.

So, while I had been missing, my mother had been out searching through the darkened cemetery, the staff were preparing for the worst, and my friends were distraught and in trouble. Yet none of this trauma impinged upon my ser-enity. I calmly handed back the syringe, I profusely and genuinely apologised for the distress caused, and I sincerely assured everybody that the crisis had brought me to my senses. They had been right, I had been wrong. The accident was in the past, and it was, after all, just an accident. From now on I would embrace life and leave the past alone.

For the next few days I was the model of recovery and co-operation. I spent time with my mother and Jayne, I participated in the therapy groups, I answered lots of questions about my plans for the future — I was everybody's shining success. And none of it mattered, none of it touched me, because close to my bosom I held the real truth of my success; I was giving myself to Margaret Healy.

I'd managed to convince Mum that I was returning to Surfers Paradise on the Queensland Gold Coast. She knew that I'd been relatively happy there, so it didn't seem unreasonable for me to want to go back. I bought my ticket and proudly displayed it to all at the ward. To them it represented proof that I had been brought back from the abyss; to me it guaranteed a journey into paradise, into a place where my guilt could be given free reign.

It didn't seem as though I was preparing for my own death, rather it was like planning a much-anticipated journey to an exciting destination. That my death would be the cost of the ticket was unimportant; and anyway it wasn't as if 'I' would be dying, merely my body. The experience of the evening trials had already proven to me the truth of our immortality; I was only present at the trials in spirit, not body, but I functioned in exactly the same way. I still had thoughts and feelings, I still had the capacity of speech, and I still had the sense of being embodied, albeit not physically. So there was little to lose and much to gain.

The most alluring aspect of crossing the threshold of death was returning to the fierce honesty and unsentimental nature of the angels. They knew all my faults, all my guilt, all my shame, and yet they were resolutely on my side. I knew that no matter what ensued from the encounter with Margaret Healy, the angels would be there to guide and support me. Even if this act resulted in the possibility of being permanently confined to the ravine, it didn't deter me because I knew that the angels also occupied that space. The demons might claim me, but never would the angels give up their quest to give me back the possibility of redemption. Of that much I was unshakeably certain.

It must have been something of this resolute certainty that convinced Mum and Dr P. not to obstruct my plans. So, after saying my farewells at the ward, I caught the train to Central Station and deposited my bags in a locker. I then caught a bus back to the suburb I used to live in, and went to the office of the GP who had previously diagnosed thrush and glandular fever. I'd phoned his office some days previously to make an appointment, and had also checked the phone book for another nearby GP and made a second appointment there.

I told each of these doctors exactly the same story. I said I'd recently begun working evening shift in a bar and was having difficulty sleeping through the daytime so needed some sleeping tablets. I specifically asked for Mandrax tablets, saying I'd used them before. Mandrax tablets were becoming popular in the clubs as a downer, and I remembered the woman pharmacist, whom I worked for briefly, expressing some concern about the recreational use of such a dangerous drug. 'Just a handful of them could kill a fully grown man,' she'd said.

Neither of the doctors raised any concerns about my request, so, emboldened, I also asked for scripts of Polaramine, a powerful anti-histamine that I used to take for a cat allergy. One tablet used to make me terribly drowsy, so it seemed to me that taking scores of them would help my cause. I then took the prescriptions from the first doctor to a nearby chemist, and afterwards caught the ferry to Manly, where I found a second chemist and handed the remaining scripts to him.

The early evening darkness had already set in as I went to a local milk bar, bought a large container of milk, and then walked to the Manly beachfront. (I still have to smile at the absurdity of buying the milk. It arose from years of hearing my mother say, 'When taking tablets, always take them with milk to protect your stomach lining.' Yes, Mum.) My 'death bed' was a wooden bench seat situated just a few steps from the edge of the sand. I was wearing some of my favourite items of clothing that had been bought with the Munich money; my 'Merivale' black leather jacket, denim jeans, and my blue suede boots. I looked down at my attire and felt pleased to be looking good as I prepared to depart this world.

For a while I sat peering into the blackness, listening to the pounding of surf on the shore, remembering the first joyful occasions of feeling my body immersed in the salty freshness of Sydney's beautiful beaches. I was grateful that I had experienced some of life's great pleasures, but I was also extremely relieved that I was now departing.

The Mandrax were largish capsules, blue I think, and as I placed handfuls of 6–8 at a time in my mouth, I recall feeling amazed at how easy it was to swallow them. The Polaramine were small, red, oval-shaped tablets, easy peasy to swallow. When all was done, which probably took less than a minute, I got up to dispose of the wrappers in a rubbish bin only a few steps away, but by the time I turned around, my legs were already shaky. I made it back to the bench just in time to feel myself losing consciousness. It was a gloriously peaceful moment. Death was immeasurably welcome.

*

Around twelve hours later, an early morning jogger noticed my pale, slumped form, and called an ambulance. The ambulance crew discovered a cold body with no pulse and no breath, but no sign of rigor mortis. It was later described to me how they took a gamble that my coldness was caused by exposure to the weather rather than as an indication of pro-longed cessation of life, and so, on nothing more than an act of faith, they began resuscitation. It seems that although exposure to the cold can hasten or cause death, it also has a preserving effect on the body that can enable successful resuscitation to take place within a greatly extended time range. Ironic, given that I'd chosen the beach for the very reason that if the pills didn't work, exposure to the cold would.

I don't know how long it took for vital life signs to reappear, but the crew did their job successfully and I was taken to the intensive care ward at Manly Hospital. No doubt heroic and exemplary care was bestowed on me during the ensuing three day coma, but, upon regaining consciousness, I'm sorry to say I had no gratitude whatsoever for their efforts. Instead I felt cheated and resentful.

The first few hazy moments of awakening were sublime; the white-clad, out-of-focus figure moving before me could easily have been an angel. My heart soared; I'd made it! Then, too quickly, almost too brutally to grasp, I heard the words, 'What's your name? If you can hear me, tell me your name.' No! No! No! This can't be true! It can't be happening! My anguished moans of, 'I don't want to be alive,' attempted to blot out the horror of realization, while simultaneously I groped for a way to avoid answering her question.

They didn't know my name because I'd intentionally removed all identification to ensure that my family would never be told about my decision. There was certainly an element of hostility in this act, but the predominant motivation was protection. I wanted them protected from the inevitable pain, but I also wanted myself protected from their anguish and grieving. I couldn't cope with any more pain; not feeling it, not causing it, not seeing it.

'Is there anyone you want me to contact?' Her question pierced my mind like a scream piercing the silence. 'Yes!' In that split second all the pain, anger, misery, hope, failure and disappointment of the past two years focused on the one person whom I'd specifically reached out to for help. Dr P., my psychiatric consultant, the only person who could have reasonably been expected to have any skills in dealing with such a mammoth crisis and trauma. Yet after being in his care for over two months I was now in a worse position than before.

I gave the nurse the name of my psychiatrist and cried out, 'And you can tell him, he's a lousy fucking doctor!' Of course, the sub-text of my message was, 'I'm desperately frightened and I don't know anybody else who might be able to understand that. Please ask him to help me.' But somehow I don't think he heard that part of the message. Thankfully, unconsciousness claimed me again, freeing me from any reflection on the consequences of my answer, leaving me unaware of the nurse's response.

As I write, I'm seeing two opposing versions of this moment of awakening from the coma. The angry response, as described, is the picture that has always appeared to me whenever I reflect back over the event, but now I find another image surfacing: of myself immediately sinking into resigned despair, giving up my name without protest, and asking for the consultant to be contacted as a way of dutifully advising him of my foolishness. Which is true? I suspect both versions capture something of the truth of that moment.

It's a new and risky enterprise for me to dare to look upon this moment without the self-protection that anger provides. With anger surging through me I can take the self-righteous stand and condemn those who violated my sovereign right to make the ultimate decision about my life, my fate. But with hurt bursting my heart and flooding my eyes I can only feel the desperate need we all have to be loved and accepted, even when, especially when, we can no longer love ourselves.

Throughout this whole sorry saga, there was only one occasion when I felt the eyes of love looking upon me. It was when I regained consciousness for the second time, and found myself in an ambulance being transferred to North Ryde Mental Hospital. Nobody had spoken to me about the transfer; in fact nobody had spoken to me at all apart from the terse exchange with the nurse. It was left to the ambulance officer to confirm my fears when I asked him if we were going to Ryde. He spoke to me tenderly, compassionately, and treated me as a worthy equal to himself. His voice, his look, and his manner all indicated care and concern for me. There was no judgement, no emotional detachment, and no advice. Just a few precious moments of holding my hand and sharing my fear about what was to come.

However, the urgency with which I was transferred, and the terror to which I was hurtling, combined to distract me from asking myself one very important question: Had I achieved my aim of meeting with Margaret Healy? The question was fated to remain deeply buried for many years yet.

At some point I lost consciousness again in the ambulance, so have no memory of my arrival at Ryde. However, my first moment of awareness was both brutal and frightening. I awoke to find a large male figure leaning over me, the shock of which was immediately eclipsed by a terrible stabbing pain in my left arm. 'My arm's hurting!' I called out, but don't remember his response. It was then that I realized my arm was bent across my body and recalled that I had a drip needle in my arm. I'd become aware of the drip needle whilst in the ambulance and had asked for it to be taken out, but was told that my condition wasn't yet stabilized so the needle had been left there as a precaution. I had no choice but to accept that, although its presence in my arm felt savage and abusive.

'There's a drip needle in my arm!' I insisted, 'I need to straighten my arm, it's hurting!' At the time it didn't occur to me to question what was preventing me from straightening my arm, all I was concerned about was easing the pain, but now it seems reasonable to assume that I had been placed in a restraining device. The idea of a fully grown man feeling the need to place a slip of a girl into a restraining device defies credibility, but then so does just about everything that I experienced at Ryde.

Did he take the needle out? I don't know, I soon lost consciousness again. The needle was gone by the time I next awoke, but I've no idea how much time had elapsed. The vein was badly bruised and very painful for weeks afterwards, and to this day the scarring on that vein prevents any blood being drawn from it.

At some stage, presumably after my condition had stabilized, I was transferred from the arrival ward to a closed ward. A peculiarly surreal memory is associated with this move; I think it's a genuine one, though it has some strange aspects associated with it. Whether they are the result of my state of mind, the after-effects of the drugs, or a consequence of treatment, who can say?

I recall sitting on a vinyl bench seat in what seemed like a waiting room, with perhaps five or six other patients. I was dressed in a hospital gown, but don't recall what the others were wearing. A nurse gave me a bowl of cornflakes and milk that were heavily smothered in white sugar, and gestured to me to eat. I sat holding this bowl in my hands and while staring into it tried to resolve a couple of troubling thoughts. The first involved my concern at the inappropriateness of eating cornflakes while sitting in a waiting room; the second involved my shock at the amount of sugar on the cornflakes. My mother had never allowed me to put that much sugar on and I wasn't sure what the consequences of eating it might be. Neither was I sure of the consequences of not eating it, so I raised a spoon to my mouth.

Just then I looked up to see Mum and Jayne entering the room; the spoon was already in my mouth, I'd been caught out. There was no choice other than to swallow. Mum stayed close to the door, watching me, but Jayne came over and sat down, enviously eyeing the cornflakes and remarking, 'Wish I could have that much sugar on mine.' I ate a couple more spoonfuls but found the sweetness overpowering. Meanwhile, Mum still kept her distance. I knew that she found the pathetic nature of the situation unbearable and was feeling aghast at the wretched state she found me in; I also knew that it would take her a long time to forgive me or ever trust me again. The nurse collected the bowl, gathered the patients together, and led us off to another destination. Did any of this happen? I can't be absolutely sure, but it feels as though it did.

The ward I was taken to had multiple beds but the number is lost to me, between four and six perhaps. Sometimes it seems like a few, sometimes a lot. My two clearest memories of the ward are of the stark bareness of the bathroom that had no cubicle doors and no shower curtains; and the stifling presence of the nurses' station outside the door of the ward. I also clearly remember the degrading humiliation of having to wear a hospital gown. It was a nasty shock to be told that I had to remain in the hospital gown they provided, though the seriousness of it didn't really sink in until they told me to go to the dining room for lunch. 'Like this!' I said. But there was something in the nurse's eyes that prevented me arguing further.

As it turned out, the dining room was filled with other shuffling apparitions in hospital gowns, so I felt quite in vogue. Inside the door of the dining room, a nurse sitting at a table beckoned me over. 'Name?' she said, without looking up. My first, totally ridiculous assumption was that she was checking to make sure I was a legitimate patient who was entitled to eat in the hospital dining room. Wrong! She scanned down the page, found my name, and gave me some pills to take. 'What are these for?' I asked. She gave me a withering look, as if to say, 'Haven't you learnt your lesson yet, fool!' I took the pills and dutifully shuffled over to get my meal. It was the first meal I had eaten in a week or more, but I don't recall a single detail of it.

The ward had a routine that included a group therapy session each weekday morning, though it is surely a monumental abuse of the English language to attach the word 'therapy' to this abomination. The duty staff (four or five) and the patients (around 20) gathered each morning in a large room, sat in a circle, and talked. It took the same form as the morning therapy group at RNH, but after a while I realized that we only discussed things that were happening on the ward, like the recreational facilities, menus, visiting arrangements etc. Nobody talked about the reasons that had brought them there in the first place!

Later I spoke with one of the nurses about my observation of the morning sessions and she replied that it was best if patients talked to their doctors about such things. Only then did it occur to me that I didn't have a clue who my doctor was. I hadn't spoken to a doctor since arriving. When I finally did have my first meeting with a doctor, it wasn't with a psychiatrist, but with a medical doctor who gave me a physical check-up.

During the examination, the doctor referred to the 'narcotic overdose' that I had taken, saying he hoped this experience had taught me not to play with recreational drugs. When I told him that it wasn't a 'narcotic overdose', but a wilful, intentional suicide involving a combination of Mandrax and Polaramine, obtained on prescription, he got agitated saying that the lab results didn't confirm my story. 'And anyway,' he said, 'if you had taken the amounts you have just described to me, you wouldn't be sitting there telling the tale.' He then dismissed me.

I pondered on this for a while, and concluded that every staff member I had encountered had avoided talking about my suicide attempt. I realized that nobody had asked for any details about what I had done or why I had done it. Moreover, the medical doctor had strongly indicated that he considered my overdose to be nothing more than a mistake resulting from playing with narcotics. Playing with narcotics!!!

The more I thought about this, the angrier I got. And the

angrier I got, the clearer my mind became. The chemically induced mental fog was lifting by the minute. I looked at the other patients, my compatriots, and saw the terrible deception that was being perpetrated on us. We were not being offered healing, support or honesty. Instead, we were being programmed into an attitude of denial. Denial both of pain and of self, a denial so insidious that the only possible outcome was annihilation. Not physical annihilation, but mental and emotional annihilation. We were being taught to completely disconnect from our true selves.

With my mind now clear about the culture and attitude that I was confronting, I sought out a nurse to demand a meeting with my, as yet unsighted, psychiatrist. Surprisingly, she told me that I was already scheduled to meet my psychiatrist the following day for an assessment of my status. At the time, I had no idea what a status assessment was; I presumed it was an assessment of my mental state. Not at all. I later discovered that it was my legal status that was under review. Committing patients involuntarily to mental hospitals requires certain stringent legal procedures to be followed, or rather, it should. In my case, committing a semi-conscious 19-year-old, who had just awoken from a 3-day coma, and who had no opportunity to be involved in the decision, probably fell well outside the guidelines. But hell, I didn't even know I was committed, let alone know what my rights were!

Later that evening, while brushing my teeth in the communal bathroom that had no doors or shower curtains, I was mulling over what to say to the psychiatrist. By chance, my eye caught sight of the moon through the high, narrow windows and I suddenly realized I hadn't gazed at the night sky for what seemed an aeon of time. I then found that by squeezing down between the basin and the shower wall, I could get quite a good upward view of the moon. It was so lovely that I lost all sense of time, and with it all sense of urgency. I barely noticed the brisk footsteps that came in and out of the bathroom, or paid any attention to the strident mutterings of staff as they hurried up and down the corridor.

Some time later I broke free of my reverie and wandered out of the bathroom towards my bed. Two young male nurses, not much older than I was, and whose attitude I had previously found to be insufferably superior, almost leapt across the nurses' desk and demanded to know where I had been. It appeared that I had been 'missing' for almost an hour. The brisk footsteps belonged to staff looking for me. Somehow I had wedged myself into a blind spot which prevented them from seeing me. My protests of innocence fell on deaf ears and I was angrily ordered to bed, but not before the two male nurses, with great delight, informed me that my behaviour would be reported to my psychiatrist ahead of tomorrow's meeting. They assured me that I could expect to be transferred to another ward that would make the present one seem like a resort.

Next morning as I sat outside his office mentally running though the issues, I was fiercely determined to tell the psychiatrist exactly what I thought of his stinking hospital. Then, absentmindedly, I looked down and saw the tatty, faded hospital gown I was still compelled to wear. The awful smell of hospital laundry filled my nostrils and suddenly, with total clarity, I knew what I had to do.

When the psychiatrist opened his door and beckoned me in, I smiled demurely, averted my eyes, and walked slowly and meekly to the chair. I waited for him to commence talking and when he asked me to respond I sincerely apologised for my wayward behaviour. I told him how grateful I was for this opportunity to reassess my life, and I asked him to allow me to prove that I was capable of leading a normal, productive life. I even offered to continue seeing my previous psychiatrist on a regular basis. He questioned me a little about what happened at the beach, and I took the opportunity to again stress that it was a silly mistake.

The ploy worked, my release papers were signed and my clothes were returned to me. After changing back into the clothes I'd worn on the night of my suicide attempt, I walked past the nurses' station that was again attended by the two jerks from the night before. For one delicious moment they didn't recognize me. Instead of seeing a shabby, nondescript, demoralized, dehumanized creature, they saw an attractive young woman who interested them. They obviously thought I was a visitor and were looking me up and down appreciatively when I shattered their demeanour by asking them whether they had lost any patients today… It was a truly satisfying moment.

1973, Perth

6

November 1973–October 1982

I was discharged into the care of my mother who had rented a small two-bedroom flat on Sydney's north shore, not far from RNS. My brother, Stephen, had been summoned back from Europe to help with the crisis, which meant Mum and Jayne shared one bedroom while Steve and I had the other, so the flat was a bit squashed.

I still have good visual recall of the flat, but my memory of the period following the discharge from North Ryde is utterly vacant. The medical records show that I visited the Cummins Unit a total of seven times after discharge, but reading the accounts doesn't raise a flicker of recognition in me; it's like reading about somebody else. The first memory that's clearly available to me occurs some three months after discharge, on 12 January 1974, my twentieth birthday. This is the day I started work as a telephonist at Sydney's then most popular television station, Channel 10. You might wonder at the implausibility of walking straight into a job such as this given my immediate history, but nothing could have been easier. I simply phoned them up, asked if there were any vacancies, and within a few days found myself employed.

There was a fantastic camaraderie amongst the staff and a lot of drunken socializing, most of which took place at the 729 Club, a members-only club for television staff and personalities. There was nothing very special or inviting about the aesthetics of the club, which comprised a bar, a lounge, a restaurant, and a gaming machine room (one-armed bandits), but it was somehow compulsive to be there. There was a sense in which working in television meant that you were no longer part of the larger community; you were different, elite, and therefore could only socialize with your own.

Once again I was back working the late shift, 3pm–11pm, and so spent a lot of time at the 729 Club. Fortunately, my other colleagues on the switchboard were married with children, so it suited all of us to let me have most of the late shifts. Of course, this meant I was living a completely different life to the previous year but it was just the right kind of atmosphere in which to test my new resolve of never speaking about my past. Nobody ever, ever got into deep and meaningful conversations. We just lived as though life was a party.

To the eyes of my family I was now, more or less, completely back to normal. Soon Steve returned to Perth, followed several months later by Mum and Jayne. My 'progress' continued unabated with the offer to be trained as a 'vision mixer' in the studios. It was a fantastic opportunity, which I jumped at. The vision mixer sits beside the director operating a console that places on screen whatever vision the director calls for, be it camera, video, graphics, special effects etc. It placed me at the heart of television productions such as drama, news, current affairs, and entertainment shows. It was wonderful and I loved it; but then a strange thing started to happen. I realized that people had started to like me. And they started to recognize that I had talent; they started to encourage me to use it. This should have been a tremendous boost to my self-esteem, but it wasn't, it only served to reinforce the lie that I was leading, the lie of pretending, once again, that I didn't have a dark secret. Couldn't they see I was a fraud; couldn't they see it was wrong for me to enjoy life, to be successful?

The obvious answer is no, they couldn't see it, and why should they? Outwardly, my life was fantastically good. Anybody looking at my behaviour at work or when socializing would have seen a genuinely happy, inspired, enthusiastic individual. But in the dark, in the solitary loneliness of the night, my thoughts would return to beings that had once asked me to account for my motives. I knew I was still watched by them, knew I always would be, and moreover, I knew that in their eyes I was a fraud. Never could I have stood before them and justified the deception I was now perpetrating.

So, after eighteen months, I resigned from the giddy world of television and began a long odyssey of wandering in the (metaphorical) wilderness. I moved constantly, changed jobs frequently, and tried to keep people at a distance. It didn't always work of course; there are many wonderful people in the world and sometimes I'd unwittingly get too close to them or they too close to me. But soon enough the urge to move on would come upon me and without a backward glance I'd be off somewhere else. The need to keep silent about the darkness of my past and the dread of what might happen if I dared to speak prevented me from seeing or caring about how my behaviour might have affected others.

And yet, despite the obvious flight aspect of this behaviour, there was also a definite sense of seeking something; a sense of needing to continue a journey. It was as though some kind of inner compass kept me moving towards an unnamed, unknown destination. It was the beginning of the long journey back to myself. The place of desolation into which I had descended was slowly beginning to release me. I'd experienced an almost complete disintegration of self since the accident, but the part of me that hadn't disintegrated, the part that had held true to the deeper, enduring mysteries of life and death was being led slowly, steadily, though circuitously, into the wondrous process of re-establishing the self.

The destination towards which I was relentlessly but unconsciously heading was a place of reconciliation with self. The journey of getting there, however, can more accurately be called collisions with self. There have been many occasions over the thirty years since the accident when my determination to live life, without reference to the accident or any of its consequences, hasn't been as easy as might first be thought. Oh, it was simple enough to remain silent, there was ample incentive for that, but I hadn't reckoned on it being my destiny to be repeatedly exposed to issues and experiences that would involve yet more encounters with death.

One such encounter occurred when, at age 23, I moved to Israel to live on a kibbutz in Caesarea, which was only a short distance from where a shocking massacre took place during an incursion by Palestine Liberation Organisation (PLO) terrorists on 11 March 1978, in which 37 Israelis died and 76 were wounded.

The decision to abandon my life in Australia for life on an Israeli kibbutz arose from reading Leon Uris' book, *Exodus*, an epic account of the establishment, in 1948, of the state of Israel. His description of the heroism of the Israelis provided stark contrast to the nightly news reports of horrendous terrorism perpetrated against Israel by the PLO.

In 1977, the media were presenting the PLO as marauding, barbarian terrorists from Lebanon who were intent on inflicting harm and suffering upon the Israelis. Few people questioned this scenario, least of all me. So much so that it was my intention to convert to Judaism and dedicate myself to the cause of protecting Israel.

Yet, when I actually arrived in Israel, which was only two weeks before the aforementioned attack, I was struck by the number of desperately poor peasants who lived near the kibbutz. They were usually elderly, dressed in black, used donkeys for transport, and were clearly deeply demoralized. After observing them for a while it became clear that they had nothing to do with the kibbutz, and that the kibbutz wanted nothing to do with them.

One day I asked the Israeli manager who these people were. He spat out the words, 'They are scum! They are Palestinians.'

'What!' I wasn't sure whether I was mortified at the thought of terrorists being so close to the kibbutz or at the thought that such obviously desperate people could be considered a threat. 'Well how did they get here?'

'They live here, but not for much longer.' The tone in his voice told me to drop the conversation, but I couldn't have continued anyway. It was suddenly obvious to me that the Palestinian situation was deeply complex. I had many questions, but asking them was clearly unsafe. Instead, I withdrew inside myself, feeling very uncertain about this path I had embarked on.

Then, a day or two later, the massacre occurred. In a statement to the press the next day, Israeli Prime Minister Begin, described the carnage inflicted by the eleven terrorists:

> ... they landed [at a beach] around Caesarea, met a young lady, questioned her, and killed her. They then proceeded – eleven in number – to the main road. They captured a taxi and killed the passengers. Then they captured a bus and ordered the driver to proceed in the direction of Tel Aviv.
>
> En route they saw another bus ahead of them. They

ordered the wounded driver to speed up and reach and overtake the second bus. When they reached that second bus, they opened fire upon it, and killed and wounded other civilians. Then they alighted from their bus to the bus they overpowered, and forced the passengers of the other bus to leave it and go into the first bus which was already under the control of the killers.

Ultimately, they reached the Country Club, and there the road was blocked. They used their arms all the time, upon vehicles passing on both sides, killing and wounding people. Ultimately, when the bus was burned as the result of an explosion, probably by a hand grenade thrown by one of the killers, the *Hevra Kadisha* [burial society] found in the bus 25 bodies, burned so that they are not recognizable and we don't know yet their identities.

This brutal massacre was made all the more shocking because the terrorists travelled from Lebanon in harmless rubber dinghies, mocking Israel's elaborate security precautions. Hardly was there time to take in the horror of what had happened, when before my eyes another horror began to manifest. The Israelis began to arm themselves and immediately spoke of vengeance. A collective lust for blood is an ugly thing to see, even when, perhaps especially when, it arises from blood already spilt.

Initially it was thought that a terrorist had jumped from the bus just prior to the explosion, and, as it took place in the immediate vicinity of the kibbutz, we were placed under a curfew. Of course, the idea of an escaped terrorist in the area only served to fan the flames of vengeance, but all I could think of was the peasants on their donkeys. What chance would they have against an armed, grieving, raging Israeli hell-bent on revenge. For me the answer was clear. The blood lust of vengeance was not an option I could support. As soon as the curfew was lifted I left Israel and returned to London, where I'd been for the previous two months.

I travelled courtesy of a plane ticket provided by a young man whom I'd met in London only a few weeks before going to Israel. He had asked me to keep in touch with him and we had coincidentally previously arranged for me to phone him on the very day of the massacre; but when I didn't phone because of the curfew he became concerned for my welfare. When I finally did get through to him, his first words were, 'Come back, I've bought a ticket for you.' I returned to London in a state of such devastation that for the next month or so I was racked by illness, and was cared for by this young man, Paul, whom I hardly knew. Nine months later I married this kind Englishman and then, two days after the ceremony, returned with him to Australia, believing that my fortunes had begun to change.

But just three weeks after we married, Paul's father died of a heart attack. His mother had died two years earlier from cancer, which meant Paul's three younger sisters (11-year-old twins and a 14-year-old) were now orphaned. We returned to London to care for them and to apply for permission to bring them back to Australia with us, which was granted twelve months later. And so, married life began amid the wreckage of death.

Nor was the wreckage confined only to Paul's family. A couple of weeks after we arrived back in London, my brother Steve phoned me with news that Jayne, my sister, had been involved in a serious car crash and wasn't expected to live. Both Steve and Mum assumed that I would fly straight back to

Perth, but for me that simply wasn't an option; it felt necessary to remain with my new family. Fortunately, Jayne made a good recovery, thanks in no small part to Mum's dedicated care. However, it took a little while longer for my decision to be forgiven.

And so death continued to intrude into my life, its presence and its effects were everywhere around me. I allowed myself the odd moment of reflecting on what business death and I had with each other, but largely my life was simply a matter of getting on with living. It's probably true to say, though, that some part of me was still not wholly reconciled with being brought back to life. I was going through the motions, and in many ways was quite happy with my life, but there was a dullness, a sadness in my soul that had become so much a part of me I hardly noticed it.

Then, in November 1980, soon after arriving back in Australia with Paul and his sisters, something quite unexpected happened. A dormant part of me woke up and once again felt the presence of the spiritual realms. It was the strangest experience; one moment I was spiritually asleep, then the next I was awake. The sensation was not unlike waking up in the morning, having a few moments of drowsiness and then suddenly remembering something from the day before. Only in this case, the day before was almost a decade past.

Nor was it a case of having forgotten my spiritual experiences. Not at all, I could remember them, but I couldn't feel them as a living reality. It was akin to the difference between remembering the feel of warm sun on your skin, and actually having warm sun on your skin. When the feeling came back it was like receiving the kiss of life.

This time the experience was not frightening, traumatic or

in any sense threatening. I was not torn from my body and hurled into a spiritual domain; no, this encounter was as mild as the other had been brutal. It came in the form of a wafting zephyr that refreshed and revived me. I wasn't seeking this kind of experience, and probably, had somebody asked me, I might have said that I didn't want it to awaken again.

The first consequence of this awakening was to become aware of the presence of a particular spiritual being. There was no visual presence, but I could receive the thoughts and intentions of this being, and I knew that it was aware of mine. In some ways, this was the opposite of being in the presence of human beings in the sense that our ability to read the inner life of other people is practically non-existent: we see them physically, but can only speculate about their thoughts and feelings, and they about ours. These barriers simply don't exist on the spiritual plane.

The reawakening of these experiences was fortunately quite gentle. I became aware of certain decisions that had to be taken, and some light was shed on certain aspects of my destiny, but it wasn't yet appropriate to speak openly of them. In many ways my life continued unchanged. Soon afterwards, however, I became pregnant with my daughter Meegan. Then, as if mirroring the immense changes taking place in my body, life suddenly became a flurry of confusion, chaos and uncertainty.

It began when Paul was turned down for a job with the Perth Fire Brigade that we assumed he was certain to get. He was previously a fire fighter with the London Fire Brigade, so when we were granted court approval to take his sisters to Australia he wrote to the Perth Brigade to ask about his chances of getting work with them. They wrote a very encouraging reply, which seemed to state that he was virtually guaranteed a position.

Upon arriving in Perth he had a couple of phone conversations with the recruitment office, which were of typically matey, chummy-type talk. They were apologetic that he would have to wait for the yearly intake quota to be advertised before they could process his application, but given that the delay only involved a few weeks it hardly mattered. However, when he hand-delivered his application form, he thought he sensed a change of attitude, but tried to dismiss it from his mind.

Alarm bells should have rung when he was informed that he would now be required to participate in all the preliminary testing procedures that applicants are asked to undergo in order to eliminate the unfit and the unworthy. Paul did note that this seemed strange, but given that he was supremely confident of passing it didn't bother him unduly. Sure enough he did pass with flying colours, and he was selected as one of eighteen final candidates for a total of thirteen positions.

In the final stage of the process, the panel of commissioners interviewed all the candidates, but unusually, prior to the interviews, candidates had been asked to submit current photographs of themselves. We tried not to read anything into this. However, towards the end of the interview, which Paul felt had gone really well, he was asked, 'How do you think you'll cope being the only black face in the force?'

He replied, 'In London, I was one of six black faces out of a force of 6,000. Here I'll be one face out of 600. It won't be a problem for me.'

Apparently though, it was a problem for most of the commissioners, because he didn't get the job for which he came highly recommended. A friend of my brother, who was a journalist, became so incensed by this that he started digging around. He claims to have spoken to one of the commissioners who admitted that the decision was made on purely racist grounds. But Paul refused to let him run the story.

Racism and bigotry were not new experiences for Paul; being born in London of mixed-race unmarried parents in 1956 meant that he had already seen more than his fair share of human ugliness. As a child of nine or ten he had to endure the humiliation of knowing that a public petition was going around to prevent his parents buying a house in a middle-class area of London. His way of coping with prejudice was not to respond to it, in the hope that depriving it of attention would eventually cause it to wither away.

By now, I was four months pregnant. Paul's two youngest sisters were thirteen; the elder sister, now almost eighteen, decided she was ready to take flight by herself and try living in Sydney. This gave Paul the idea of applying to the Sydney Fire Brigade for a position. So, he rang them up, had a nice chummy chat, and was told, 'We're recruiting now, we'd love to get an application from you.' We put our house on the market, packed up all our belongings, gave notice at the girls' school, and left Perth two weeks later, leaving our empty house in the hands of an agent. We also left Paul's sisters in the care of friends until we had found suitable accommodation in Sydney.

But, a week later, we'd abandoned our plans and were back in Perth. Paul had gone into the recruitment office, asked for the person he spoke to on the phone, then watched the man's facial contortions as he tried to reconcile the 'mate' he'd spoken to with the black face standing before him. Something in Paul changed during that encounter: he went into that office a hopeful man but he came out of it a bitter one, refusing to even lodge his application form.

This incident was also to have a drastic effect on Paul's sisters. Not only were they deeply disappointed about not joining their elder sister, but also they had to face the embarrassment of returning to a school they had just left. Unfortunately, most of their anger about this was directed at me for the simple reason that I returned to Perth a week ahead of Paul. He was driving back, but I returned by plane.

Then, just to complicate matters further, when Paul finally did arrive back, he announced that he wanted to live in Melbourne! He'd had the bright idea of driving back to Perth via Melbourne and Adelaide so that he could get the feel of them; but the feel he got for Melbourne was love at first sight. Therefore, while the girls and I made some semblance of settling back into our lives, Paul was avidly reading the employment pages of the Melbourne papers. And sure enough, before long he found just what he was looking for, an advertisement for Emergency Service Workers with the Port of Melbourne Authority.

It wasn't quite fire-fighting work, but it was close enough. He went to Melbourne for an interview, and came back with the news that we were on the move again. By now I was almost eight months pregnant. Once again we packed up our belongings, took the girls out of school, and put the house back on the market. This time though, the atmosphere was fraught and tense. Paul was wound up, the girls were resentful, and I was rapidly feeling out of my depth in continuing to care for them.

During the following six weeks all the effort that had been put into caring for the girls through the previous two years simply evaporated. I was exhausted, Paul was distracted, and they were sullen. My due date was now only a couple of weeks away. In desperation for some respite I told Paul that he would have to give up playing cricket two nights a week to spend more time with the girls. He refused. I countered by saying that I could no longer manage; either he carried more of the burden or the girls would have to go into care.

The words were out of my mouth before I realized what I was saying but once out there was no putting them back. In that moment I knew that I couldn't go on and from the speed with which Paul acted on my words, it clearly was the same for him. It was one of the saddest moments of my life, and one of the few decisions about which I feel genuine regret; and yet, on another level, I know that this is the way it had to be. Had we sought help sooner, things might have been different.

Meegan, in her wisdom, decided she was going to stay put in the womb for as long as possible so she didn't see the light of day until twelve days past her due date. Her birth, in September 1981, continued and consolidated the sense of spiritual awakening that had happened a year earlier. At first the process was largely an unconscious one, I was simply an adoring mother who couldn't take my eyes off the miracle that lay before me. Yet the more that I watched, and the more that I adored and marvelled, the more did my eyes begin to 'see'.

I could 'see' that Meegan's physical growth was not just a matter of rapidly replicating cells, but that those cells were replicating because of an elaborate weaving and inter-penetrating of spiritual forces that were working into physical matter. I could look into her eyes and 'see' an intelligence that demanded respect. I could watch the way she engaged with the world and 'see' an emerging confidence that was born of familiarity.

The more I saw these things in Meegan, the more I saw them in myself, in others, and in the world. I could even look on all the turmoil of the past months and see that some good might emerge from it. In fact, good was coming from it, the girls were visiting regularly and seemed to be getting something positive out of the new situation. I had even been moved to contact my mother and make gestures of reconciliation. And Paul and I were moving on from what might have been an unhealable fracture between us.

Then, out of the blue, came a bolt of lightning from the other direction. I awoke one night to the frightening sensation of being pulled upwards in a spiralling manner. There was some similarity with the way in which I used to be summoned to the ravine courtroom, but whoever was doing the pulling this time didn't have nearly the same power as the previous beings.

Once I became aware of what was happening, I inwardly called out, 'No! I'm not coming to you.' With that, everything became quiet again; everything, that is, except the pounding of my heart. It was the first time in over ten years that such a thing had happened; I lay in bed trying to quell the panic, knowing that remaining calm was my only defence. As soon as my legs felt able to carry me I went into Meegan's room to check on her; she was sleeping soundly. Paul was working night shift and wouldn't be home for hours, so, as before, I lay alone in the darkness wondering what might come next.

Nothing happened the next night or the night after that; and when a few more nights had passed without occurrence I had all but stopped thinking about it. Then, my mother phoned to say she had just been informed that my father had died a week ago. Was it his crossing of the threshold that I experienced? I don't know, but it's a possibility.

Dad had never resumed contact with the family after he left

Perth following the accident, yet he named my mother as his superannuation beneficiary, which is why the authorities informed her of his death. They told her that he had died on Christmas morning 1981, aged 52, from the effects of a stroke he'd suffered 12 months earlier. He had lived in Adelaide for the whole of the ten years that he'd been missing, working as a bus driver.

The authorities gave me the contact details of the couple who had been caring for him when he died, so in a quest for some answers I went to visit them. They told me that they had been close friends for the whole time Dad had lived in Adelaide; so when he was struck down by the stroke and confined to hospital bed care, they often brought him to their home for respite care on weekends and special occasions.

They then described how, after enjoying a meal together on Christmas Eve, they put Dad to bed at around midnight. They set the alarm for his 6am medication when he assured them he would manage to take it without assistance. The next morning at 7.30am, when the children awoke to open their presents, Dad's friend went into the bedroom to bring him out for the present opening, but found him dead. His 6am medication had been taken.

We talked together for some time before I found the courage to ask them what Dad had said about me. With some embarrassment they informed me that throughout their long friendship he had never uttered a word about having a wife and three children. By way of consolation they told me that he had never remarried nor entered into another relationship.

After collecting Dad's pitifully few personal belongings, which were handed to me by the Public Trustee in an A4 manila envelope, I took them to Perth to formally acknowledge Dad's passing with my mother and siblings.

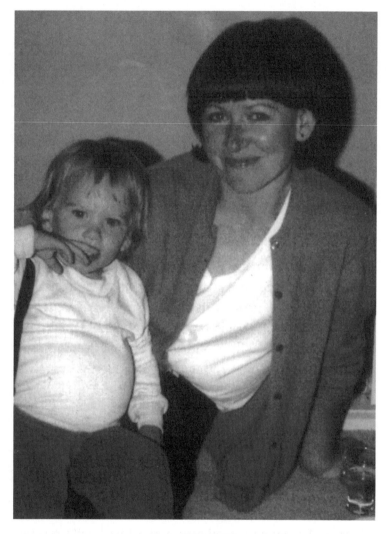

November 1983

7

1983–1991

Two months after Meegan's second birthday I told Paul the marriage was over. It was difficult to justify, both to him and to myself. In many ways he was a good and caring husband and father, yet there was something stirring in me that couldn't find expression within marriage, and it couldn't any longer be denied or suppressed. The only way to identify it was to submit to the inner compass once again.

It began with a three-month sojourn in Perth, during which time I renounced the use of my married name and reclaimed the use of my birth name. This was a partly symbolic gesture, but it was also the means by which I was able to make a concrete statement to the world about an inner commitment I'd made to stop running away from myself. This act of visiting Perth twelve years after the accident was a necessary (though at the time, unconscious) step towards integrating the experience within myself in a new way. It helped me to re-establish an independent view of life, and to feel that genuine progress had been made in my quest to feel legitimate again.

Returning to Melbourne was always on my agenda because I'd enrolled in a one-year course to be trained as a Childbirth Educator. Becoming a mother was the first totally positive experience of my life, but the birth experience was horrible. So it seemed a good idea to dedicate myself to furthering the cause of improving birthing conditions for women and babies.

The first few months of the training were fantastically stimulating. There were around 15 participants, all women, and all with some notion of wanting to bring greater autonomy to birthing parents. The training was run by the Childbirth Education Association of Victoria, which itself had some renown for wanting to radicalize the birthing process. What I didn't realize, or hadn't bothered to find out until it was too late, was that the latter part of the training included several sessions of Primal Scream Therapy.

Primal Scream is the title of a book written in the 1970s by Dr Arthur Janov, in which he describes an intensive form of therapy aimed at uncovering childhood hurts and trauma. What made this form of therapy so distinctive was that it actively encouraged people to scream out their rage and their hurt. The means of encouragement was also rather unique in that the clients, usually in groups, lay on the floor of a padded room, decorated red to replicate the womb, while therapists cajoled them into 'expressing' the inevitable store of rage that we bring with us from childhood.

Well, as you might imagine, this didn't appeal to me one little bit. However, the rationale of the course trainers was that all the participants had to take part in order to resolve the trauma that we would still be carrying from our own births. It was a case of do the therapy or fail the course. The wisest response would have been to call their bluff, but at the time that didn't occur to me. Instead, naivety kicked in, and I told the history of the accident to the course leader whom I trusted and respected. My assumption was that she would recognize the genuine nature of my reluctance to participate, and release me from the obligation. She didn't.

When the day finally arrived, all of the participants, along with two of the course leaders, were shown into a large, dark red, padded room. The floor had two levels: the first half, at the entrance to the room, was floor level, while the rear half was raised by a one-metre platform covered with the same red padding as covered the walls. At least, we were told it was red, but the lighting was so dim it might as well have been black.

After we had all settled ourselves onto the platform floor, some sitting, some sprawling, Dr Graham Farrant, the psychiatrist running the show turned on a movie projector and showed footage of some torturous births attended by horrendous medical interventions. The film concluded with scenes of adults 'primal screaming' their way through rebirthing. The purpose of this was clearly to get people in the mood, so to speak. Sure enough, some of my colleagues were already weeping and writhing long before the film ended.

We were then invited to lie on the floor and 'express' whatever had arisen in us. To assist our expression, a group of four or five assistants worked their way around the floor, provoking and cajoling responses out of us. Initially, none of the assistants came to me and I was left alone to ponder my own responses in peace, and to listen to the vigorous expressions of my group. The response that had been paramount for me was one of utter relief and gratitude that I had been privileged to have a home birth. Alongside that was a powerful feeling of needing to keep myself well protected from what was going on.

'How are you doing?' Eventually, one of the assistants, a youngish woman in her mid-twenties approached me.

'It's noisy in here,' I replied.

'Don't listen to others, make some noise yourself.'

When I didn't respond she asked, 'What are you worried about?'

'I'm wondering why you are recording this?' I said, pointing up towards what looked like a closed circuit camera.

'You're paranoid,' she said, 'that's not a camera, it's an ioniser.'

'Is it paranoid to think this might be filmed, given what we've just seen?'

'You've got a trust problem. It's time you sorted it out.'

'Well, you might be right, but your film has left me feeling pretty contented with my lot, so I think I should just enjoy it for the moment.'

'You've got no reason to be feeling content.'

'Oh?'

We parried backwards and forwards for a little while more until she revealed that she knew I had objected to coming to the session, and what's more she knew why.

This revelation might have been intended to provoke a particular reaction, but it only served to confirm that I was right to protect myself and say nothing. Then she asked me a most unexpected question, 'Have you ever wanted to meet the woman you killed?'

'Yes,' I answered, 'I have met her. We spoke when I died.'

'What did you say to her?'

'I don't have the slightest clue. All I know is that it happened.'

'Do you think she's forgiven you?'

'Yes, I know she has.'

Up until saying these words, I don't recall ever having thought about what might have taken place when I crossed the threshold. Yet the certainty with which I gave the answer left me in no doubt that it was true. We had spoken; she had forgiven me. The joy of that knowledge suffused my heart like warm sunshine. Looking up at my interrogator, I softly said, 'Fancy making a discovery like that in a place like this.'

At that point she left me alone to further reflect on my discovery. Shortly afterwards the session came to an end and we were ushered from the raised floor back to ground level. We sat on the red carpet, leant back against the red walls, and began a process of reflection guided by Graham Farrant.

He began by asking for feedback on anything that had been experienced. Quite a few responses were given, some positive, some not. When the discussion began to ebb he looked straight at me, asking, 'And what about you? For somebody who's looking so smug, you haven't had much to say.' It was true, I hadn't contributed at all. This was partly because I still wanted to hug the moment close to me; partly because I didn't feel I'd really been participating in a 'primal scream' scenario; and partly because I still felt suspicious about the process.

However, when pressed, I decided to be generous. 'I had reservations about coming here, but I'm leaving with something very positive. So thank you, it's been a very positive day.'

'A very positive day.' He repeated my words with such an edge of sarcasm to them, that I was momentarily unsure of how or whether to respond. 'You've had a very positive day,' he again repeated, 'Well then, does that mean that you are now ready to face reality?'

I looked at him blankly.

'Now that you think you've been forgiven by the woman you accidentally killed, it's time to face the reality of asking yourself who it really was that you wanted to kill.'

'What!' My mind was racing; I hadn't said anything to him about the accident or my conversation with the assistant, so where had his information come from. I glanced across the room to the course leader whom I'd previously confided in, and realized there was something of a set-up going on.

'There is no such thing as an accidental killing,' he went on, 'Every so-called accident is actually an opportunistic killing that occurs when we unexpectedly find ourselves in a situation where we can do what we've always wanted to do. Where we can fulfil our wish to kill somebody. What I'm asking you to do now, is to identify who it was you really wanted to kill.'

'You're wrong. There was nobody I wanted to kill' I replied, shocked.

'She was an older woman, wasn't she?' He asked.

'Yes.'

'Then it was probably your mother you wanted to kill. Did you see a momentary flash of your mother just before the impact?'

'No!' I was now feeling sickened by his needling.

'I don't believe you. Look at you, you're a mess. Not feeling so smug now are you' – said he, who was smugness personified.

'You can't talk to me like this. This is slanderous. I'll get you struck off for this!' I thundered.

My composure was now completely gone; I was shrieking, crying and shaking. The shame that I felt was immense; the loathing that I felt was even greater. A colleague sitting next to me took my arm and led me out of the room. She just held me while I cried and cried, telling me over and over, 'He's wrong, he's wrong.'

I knew with utter certainty that Graham was wrong. It was not an opportunistic killing; it was not a substitute killing. Nevertheless, despite his grotesque misinterpretation of the situation, my heart and mind knew that he was onto something. There was a reality that I hadn't yet faced. His targeting of me opened up the old wound, and stirred up an old question; why was my encounter with Margaret Healy so seemingly deliberate? Why was everything that happened on the morning of the accident designed to ensure that we met at the very point we did?

How ironic that Dr Graham Farrant, for all the wrong reasons, should be the one to re-open all the right questions. Mind you, it took a while for the red haze of anger and loathing to pass before these questions came into focus. They only arose into my consciousness during a conversation with a lawyer about starting legal proceeding against Graham Farrant. It was the thought of exposing all the complications around the accident that put me off proceeding; as well as the fact that the CEA announced the cancellation of future primal scream sessions.

Nothing much was ever directly said to me about the incident; presumably it was as shocking to witness as it was to experience, particularly given the degree of unawareness that my colleagues had about this part of my history. As much as possible we all just ignored it, or at least pretended to. For me, though, the die was now cast, my future did not lie in Childbirth Education. In fact I couldn't see my future path at all, other than in terms of always being at the mercy of my past.

Yet Graham Farrant wasn't the only reason for the change of heart about my vocation. There had been another profoundly affecting encounter that arose from an observation made by a visiting tutor who was listening to my description of Meegan's birth. I was complaining about the number of unnecessary interventions that had marred the experience, when she responded, 'Yes, but they only happened because of your choices.' Indignantly, I pointed out that none of the interventions were of my choice. 'That's not what I said,' she quietly persisted, 'I said they happened because of your choices.'

'Are you saying they were my fault?'

'Listen carefully to what I'm saying. I'm saying the interventions happened because of choices that you made.'

By now I was getting very hot under the collar. 'You *are* saying they were my fault! How dare you accuse me of that. It's the hospitals that are at fault, not the women who use them!'

She looked at me calmly and implacably, 'You may choose to blame others for your life, or you may choose to ask yourself, 'How did I contribute to this situation and why?' Personally I prefer to look at my role, at my behaviour, and to accept that the only person who can accept responsibility is me.'

'That's bullshit! It completely denies the reality of most people's lives. We have almost no control over life, and precious little opportunity to make deliberate choices about it! In your scenario you're talking about women being able to choose a perfect home birth with absolutely no complications. Well guess what, for most women that's not a realistic choice. Women have all sorts of reasons for wanting or needing to give birth in hospital, and we need to make that a better experience. What I'm saying is that doctors need to treat birthing women with greater dignity and respect. They were at fault in my situation, and they are at fault in most birthing situations where unnecessary intervention takes place.'

She looked at me silently for a few moments, then quietly repeated, 'The interventions happened because of choices that you made.'

My fury and frustration were at breaking point, leaving me no option other than to walk out of the session. Later, the conversation played in my head over and over. I detested the woman, and I hated every word she spoke. Why? Because I heard the truth of what she said and it was unbearable.

The course left me feeling exposed and vulnerable, so at its completion there was little else that I wanted to do except pack a bag and go travelling. The idea of travelling with a three-year-old might not be everyone's cup of tea, but Meegan was a natural adventurer. Which is just as well given that she had crossed the continent of Australia eight times, as well as travelling to England and back before she was two years old.

Meegan had another very unusual characteristic that was present from a very young age; she loved to converse with people. Even when she was pre-verbal she had an uncanny knack of drawing total strangers into conversation with her. It began when she smiled at the midwife at six days old. It continued when she would 'talk' to people in shops or on buses by squealing, cooing, or flapping her arms until the person responded. Of course this meant that the person she had targeted would talk to her through me, which in turn meant that I had suddenly to become a sociable person. Surprisingly, it was easy to do this on her behalf, whereas to do it on my own behalf was near impossible.

Once she became verbal, which as you might guess happened quite early, she was in seventh heaven. If she wasn't talking, she was singing, if she wasn't singing, she was chattering to dolls, insects or fairies, if she wasn't doing any of these, she was asleep. I loved her enthusiasm for life, for people, for stones and plants and insects, for the stars above, for the food she ate, for the day, for the night, for the sleeping time and the waking time. Meegan loved life in a way that constantly astounded me; that constantly challenged me to see the world through her eyes.

Fortunately, she ultimately proved to be the perfect counterbalance to some dark stirrings that had once again begun to haunt me. Perhaps it was predictable that choosing to immerse myself in issues surrounding the threshold of birth would inevitably draw me back towards unresolved issues concerning the threshold of death. Nevertheless, it came as a surprise to find that for the first time in ten years I felt concerned enough about myself to want to return to therapy.

Our travels had thus far taken us to the New South Wales north coast, a region renowned for alternative lifestyles, when the need to return to therapy came upon me. I headed for Lismore, the largest regional town in the area, thinking that would be the best place to find help. By a stroke of luck, minutes after disembarking from the train, my eye caught sight of a notice advertising supported accommodation for women and children in need.

It turned out to be a women's refuge, and although it was primarily intended as an escape from domestic violence, Meegan and I were invited to stay due to being technically homeless. It turned out to be a wonderful haven. The house was situated in a quiet street, close to the town centre. It was a 'Queenslander' house, which means it was built off the ground on wooden stilts three metres high, as a protection against flooding.

From the outside it looked like any other family home, but inside it was teeming with life and energy. Each of the four bedrooms was crammed with as many beds as could possibly fit, and, given that mothers and children often shared beds, as did Meegan and I, it was fit to bursting. Yet the support and camaraderie were more than enough to offset any problems that the overcrowding might bring. The positive atmosphere was partly due to the skills and the compassion of the staff, and partly due to the relief and gratitude of the residents.

Few women spoke directly about the circumstances that had led them to the refuge; instead the conversations were largely about the choices that had to be made for the future. For some that meant leaving the town they'd always lived in, for others it meant finding safe ways to stay, for almost all it meant beginning again in a new house and new school. For me, it meant finding a therapist, yet all the while avoiding talking about why I needed one. However, I did open up somewhat to the refuge staff and asked them to recommend a suitable therapist.

'Gerry' was a quiet, unassuming man in his late forties. He showed me into his office, which was fairly conventional but had a reassuring touch of homely dishevelment about it. When I had given him the basic story, he ruminated thoughtfully for a few minutes before saying, 'I have a picture before me. It's of a young man on horseback, galloping through fields without a care in the world. It's set in a time long ages past, he's wearing something akin to a toga, and he's riding bareback. Unbeknown to him a small girl, perhaps no more than four, five years old is about to cross his path. She is engrossed in the meadow flowers she has just picked; he is intoxicated by the power and freedom of the horse. Neither of them has the slightest awareness of the presence of the other. It's not until the thundering hoofs are almost upon her that they see each other. But by then it's too late. The mother of the child could see what was to happen yet neither her cries nor her running were enough to prevent the inevitable. Shrieking with grief she cradles the broken body of her daughter.

'The boy, for that is what the proud young man has again

become, sinks down on his shaky legs and looks out through his glazed, shocked eyes at his sister's limp form and his mother's unendurable agony. Before he can speak, his mother howls her rage at him, "Get away from me! Get away from me! Never come back! Do you hear me! Never come back!" The boy dragged himself away to a life of exile, knowing he would never be forgiven.'

When Gerry had finished telling this story, he looked at me expectantly, waiting for a reaction. When one didn't come, he said, 'This picture is an explanation from a previous life for your current situation. The boy in the story is your mother; the mother in the story is you. During a previous life you inflicted great harm and suffering on the person who is now your mother, so, in this life it is necessary for you to receive something similar from her. To break the cycle you must forgive her for all the hurt she has caused you.'

Listening to this incredible scenario issuing forth from a perfectly ordinary looking man using the sort of matter-of-fact, normal voice that one would use to exchange pleasantries about the weather, disarmed me somewhat. I wanted to tell him that he was a raving lunatic; I wanted to weep at the futility of once again telling my story to someone who couldn't hear it; instead, great weariness descended on me at the realization that he couldn't help me. Or rather, that I wasn't willing to accept what he was offering.

It wasn't that I was opposed to the concept of past lives, it was more a sense of not being able to accommodate anything as concrete as what he was proposing. Certainly not from the perspective of what he claimed it meant for me personally, but nor from the standpoint that it was even possible or desirable to be that precise about a past life. I declined to make another appointment with him, but I knew that something about the encounter would continue to live on in me.

Strange as it may seem, despite my experiences of meeting the spiritual world and its beings, the urge to understand this world or to study what others said about it was largely non-existent. It simply didn't occur to me to try to find corroborating accounts or to explore for meaning beyond my own comprehension. Is this arrogant? Probably. Yet primarily it's a measure of how deep an impression the encounters had made. I had no curiosity about them because I simply couldn't separate myself sufficiently from the experience to be able to look at it objectively. Yet despite wanting to reject what Gerry had said, he gave me a glimpse into a landscape that, over many years slowly, quietly, but persistently sought to be explored.

After Gerry, I went to see a youngish woman counsellor, who immediately admitted that her training had not given her any preparation for the issues that concerned me. Nevertheless, she was willing to listen, so we met five or six times before mutually agreeing to end the sessions. For me, the sessions revealed no great shifts of understanding, but they allowed me a sense of being able to unpack the load I carried, and then repack it more comfortably. Shortly afterwards I felt sufficiently composed to be able to resume travelling.

At the urging of the refuge staff I headed for the university town of Armidale, in north-west New South Wales, promising to enrol in a degree course. The town was as lovely as they had said, and the university grounds were gorgeous, but after talking to the admissions officer I knew that an academic education wasn't going to fulfil the need for knowledge that was starting to grow within me. I had no idea what I needed or wanted, but out of the blue came a familiar, powerful urge:

cross the Nullabor. So Meegan and I boarded a bus and set out on the five-day journey across the continent to Perth.

It was quite nice to be back in Perth with its clear blue sky, gorgeous beaches, hot summers, mild winters, and its laid-back, unhurried life. It was also very nice to see the way in which Mum and Meegan enjoyed each other's company. Mum and I had developed a sort of uneasy truce with each other over the years, which meant we could keep the peace so long as certain lines weren't breached. Though sooner or later one or other did breach the line, resulting in a stormy resumption of hostilities for a period, but something about that pattern began to change after Meegan was born.

It wasn't a case of the old, 'You'll understand your mother when you become a mother yourself' cliché, it was more a sense of fascination at watching the two of them together. They seemed to know each other in a completely different way than I knew them as individuals, which in turn revealed aspects of them that I'd not seen before. Mum became a much softer person around Meegan, and while that might be no more than first grandchild syndrome, it led me to conclude that they were not strangers to each other.

This conclusion wasn't directly connected with Gerry's picture, at least not consciously. In fact, Gerry had been so decisively dismissed from my mind he'd pretty much sunk into oblivion at this stage. What I saw in Meegan and Mum's connection didn't have any kind of picture or rationale attached to it; it merely existed on the level of an unconditional acceptance that some kind of bond existed between them that was independent of me or of any temporal connection.

Before long the idea of remaining in Perth began to grow on me, making it necessary to look about for a pre-school for

Meegan. Fortunately the local neighbourhood centre had organized a series of talks by representatives from a range of different schools. The presentations were from the local state school, a Catholic school, an Anglican school, a Montessori school and a Steiner school.

For me, the Steiner school was the clear choice even though I'd never heard of it previously, and even though I'd long vowed that no child of mine would go to a private, fee-paying school. What won me over was the beautiful class-room environment in which the child is reverently enfolded, and Dr Rudolf Steiner's astonishing philosophy of child development on which the curriculum is based (none of the other schools had anything even remotely approaching a philosophy).

Yet in choosing this school for Meegan I had no idea that I'd also unwittingly begun an eighteen-year journey in which the answers to the questions that had tormented me about the accident would begin to be revealed. One further serious obstacle still had to be overcome however.

The obstacle that threatened to sabotage my commitment to the Steiner school was my old nemesis, Christianity. Over the years my hostility to all religions had deepened and hardened, though it was for the Christian churches that I saved my sharpest vitriol. There seemed to me no contradiction between this and my recognition of the existence of a spiritual realm. Quite the contrary, it was because my spiritual experiences had no frame of reference within the mush that passes for Christianity that my antagonism was so great.

Imagine then my horror when at Christmas a nativity play was performed (remember, this is Australia, the western world's most secular country, where schools do not perform nativity plays). When I asked the teacher why that play had been chosen, she said, without a trace of irony, 'Because it's Christmas.'

'Yes, I realize that, but bringing this into school smacks of Christian indoctrination.'

'Did you not think it was very beautiful?'

'Of course, everything here is beautiful, it's what you specialize in, but that's not the point. You're asking these kids to believe something that's nonsense.'

'Oh, so when we tell fairy stories or sing nursery rhymes, am I also asking them to believe something?'

'Are you saying this play is just another fairy story?'

'No, but you can see it that way if you prefer.'

At this point another parent intervened, assuring me that Steiner had recommended Christianity be introduced in the pre-school because it's a story that is only suitable for childhood. 'Don't worry,' she said, 'if they get it now, it means they'll grow out of it before adolescence.' Her words were very reassuring, and of course they rang very true given that she was describing my own relationship to Christianity. The pity was that it didn't take long to discover that Steiner said no such thing.

The crunch came the following Easter when the school 'festival' proved to be an uncomfortably close replica of the Easter rituals I remembered attending at church as a child. It was too much for me. I took Meegan out of school, convinced that she was in danger of being indoctrinated by Christianity, though of course, in reality, she was never in danger; it was simply a case of my buttons being pushed.

For the next three years, secular alternative schooling provided Meegan's education. While in its own way it was fine, it did lack a sense of reverence towards childhood and learning that had so impressed me about the Steiner curriculum. When the alternative school hit a funding crisis and had to close its doors, my inclination was to give the Steiner school another try. Mind you, this only came about because another parent who was also looking for a school for her daughter described to me her very positive impressions of visiting the Steiner school.

Listening to her reports about the beautiful architecture, the gorgeous arts and crafts, the grand scope of the curriculum, the emphasis on imaginative learning rather than abstract learning and the sheer optimism inherent in the fact that throughout primary school the same teacher remains with a class for seven years, brought it all back. Yet the defining moment, which caused a yearning to well up in my heart, was being reminded of the Steiner tradition of each child being met at the classroom door with a handshake and a personal greeting from their teacher. For me, something in the simplicity of this gesture encapsulated the prime characteristic of Steiner education: the honouring and acknowledging of each child's individuality.

Settling back into the school was relatively easy since many of Meegan's original classmates remembered her and welcomed her warmly. It proved to be a good move on many fronts that heralded a very steady couple of years: not only Meegan's growth and education thrived, but also my sense of being 'educated' alongside Meegan began to develop. It was quite subtle to start with, just an awareness that my interest in and admiration for both the curriculum and its underlying philosophy were starting to take up more and more space in my thoughts.

This became possible only because I'd worked out a rational compromise with myself about the Christian influence, which I still experienced as being overly present. It was tolerable so long as Meegan showed no signs of falling under its spell. Yet it was also true to say that thanks to encountering the books of Krishnamurti I was attempting to emulate an attitude of quiet acceptance towards the more irritating aspects of life.

Krishnamurti became something of a hero of mine (probably the first I'd ever had), when I read his 1929 speech dissolving The Order of the Star in the East, an organization founded in 1911 to proclaim the coming World Teacher (the new Christ). The significance of this dissolution was that Krishnamurti was refusing to comply with the view of its followers that *he* was the World Teacher whom they had been preparing for. He said:

> You have been preparing for eighteen years, and look how many difficulties there are in the way of your understanding, how many complications, how many trivial things. Your prejudices, your fears, your authorities, your churches new and old – all these, I maintain, are a barrier to understanding. I cannot make myself clearer than this. I do not want you to agree with me, I do not want you to follow me, I want you to understand what I am saying. This understanding is necessary because your belief has not transformed you but only complicated you, and because you are not willing to face things as they are. You want to have your own gods – new gods instead of the old, new religions instead of the old, new forms instead of the old – all equally valueless, all barriers, all limitations, all crutches. Instead of old spiritual distinctions you have new spiritual distinctions, instead of old worships you have new worships. You are all depending for your spirituality on someone else, for your happiness on someone else, for

your enlightenment on someone else; and although you have been preparing for me for eighteen years, when I say all these things are unnecessary, when I say that you must put them all away and look within yourselves for the enlightenment, for the glory, for the purification, and for the incorruptibility of the self, not one of you is willing to do it. There may be a few, but very, very few. So why have an organization?*

It was music to my ears. Here was a man who knew of the existence of the spiritual realm of life yet who didn't need or want to express it within an organized framework – not even as its appointed leader! My admiration was further enhanced by the strong similarities that I perceived between the manner of Krishnamurti's pragmatism, and the 'tough love' of the angels who were present at my evening trials.

Yet, alongside the wisdom of Krishnamurti, another book, *The Essene Gospel of Peace*, began to draw my attention. This tiny book, the Aramaic original of which was allegedly found in Vatican archives by Professor Edmond Bordeaux Szekely, was first published in 1939. It recounts a meeting between Jesus and a group of sick and maimed men who ask why they have been inflicted with infirmity. Amazingly, Jesus immediately offers to open the door of life to the men by leading them into 'the kingdom of our Mother's angels'. (And just in case you think it's a misprint, I'll repeat it; 'the kingdom of our *Mother's* angels'.)

When I picked up this book I had no idea it was going to be

---

* http://www.kinfonet.org/Biography/ (This is the website of the Krishnamurti Information Network.)

about Jesus; had I known, I simply wouldn't have read it. Yet to unexpectedly encounter a Jesus who was about to describe the kingdom of the Mother's angels was electrifying. He then describes to the men, in beautifully poetic language, how every aspect of the human body is part of every aspect of the surrounding world; and that every aspect of both human and earth owes its existence to the Mother and her angels.

My heart and mind began to race: this was starting to sound like a description of my experience of the world, one imbued with ever-present spiritual activity. But something even more amazing was about to come. Jesus begins to tell these men that to heal their afflictions they must fast and they must allow the Mother's angels of air, water and sunlight to cleanse the body of all impurities. He then gives a wonderfully precise, but still poetic account of how to use a gourd to give oneself an enema. Moreover, he tells of the foul sight and stink that awaits them when the water begins to flow out.

This Jesus was growing on me by the minute. Not only was he extolling a feminist version of the kingdom, but he was also talking about something as ungodly as excrement! By the end of the book I was hooked. This was my kind of Jesus! Then, close on the heels of meeting this Jesus, came another renegade version courtesy of a book entitled *God Calling* which purports to be the result of messages from the risen Christ given to two elderly women living in England during the 1930s.

Normally I wouldn't have bothered with this book at all, but it was given to me by an older woman whom I worked with. She was clearly going to ask me for my opinion next time we met, so in order to have a prepared response I glanced through it. The book consists of short daily meditations so I naturally opened the book at the meditation for my birthday. The title for 12 January is 'Thanks for Trials'. It urges an attitude of joyful gratitude towards all that one encounters in life, even trials.

I was a bit taken aback by this because it reflected an attitude that I had been attempting to sustain since reading Shakti Gawain's book *Creative Visualisations* when I was thirty-one. One of the visualization exercises in Shakti's book involved imaginatively returning the self to a time before life started to go wrong, and then to 'imagine' oneself into another version of life. Obviously, I chose to take myself back to the day before the accident. It wasn't difficult to recall the tremendous sense of joyous empowerment and invincibility that my adolescent self felt. Nor was it difficult to envisage being driven uneventfully to work by Dad and then going out with the family to celebrate Jayne's birthday. There were no problems imagining the frenetic lead-up to the excitement of going on my working holiday; but, curiously, from that point on the exercise became increasingly fraught.

The images that came forth were of a vain, superficial life devoid of any real meaning or purpose. No matter how elevated or interesting I tried to make it, nothing could remove a pervading sense of emptiness. Finally, in a shocking moment of recognition, I realized that if the accident hadn't happened I wouldn't be who I was. With tears streaming down my face I looked at the sleeping form of Meegan and for the first time felt the connection between what is and what was. In that moment I felt absolute gratitude for everything that had happened in my life. There wasn't a single second of my life that I would have traded away.

It was a wonderful feeling to look at my daughter and to know with absolute certainty that everything had been worthwhile, that everything had purpose and meaning. The relief and joy of that moment were so strong that I can still very easily bring both the image and the feeling back to consciousness. Perhaps that's because it was not only intense but also very fleeting; for following close behind came an avalanche of shame and guilt over the perversity of feeling grateful for causing a death.

In the years since, my inner world has consisted of silently, privately, trying to find the balance between these two opposing forces, gratitude and guilt, both of which seemed to me to have equal validity. Yet curiously, despite the enormity of the inherent moral question, at no time did it occur to me to seek higher spiritual guidance. Possibly that's because my attitude to these things had been defined during the evening encounters with angels when I defiantly claimed sovereignty over my own soul. Since then, despite being all too aware of the very real presence of spiritual beings, I chose not to directly seek their engagement on any issues about the accident for fear of what it might stir up. In fact, I really didn't seek their engagement on any issues at all; I respectfully, even wondrously, acknowledged their presence and influence, but it never occurred to me to ask for their help.

Then, at age 37, there came a sudden and dramatic change. Late one evening, while reading the daily meditation in *God Calling*, the urge came upon me to engage in a 40-day silent retreat, beginning the next morning. Actually, to call it an urge is not quite correct; it was more like a demand or even a goad. My initial response was to scoff at the impracticality of it, while surprisingly also feeling a certain attraction to the sheer audacity and novelty of it. Nevertheless, the idea wouldn't be easily shaken off, so to prove to myself that it simply wasn't possible I began looking through my diary for evidence of why it couldn't be done. The evidence was bountiful, but ultimately useless because when my calculations arrived at the fortieth day, it was 18 April, the twentieth anniversary of the accident.

I experienced an immediate capitulation in my will; my mind could only surrender to the thought that some higher force or being must have orchestrated this. Moreover I was in no doubt about who that was; it was the being who spoke to me every day through *God Calling*, it was the Christ being Himself. Thus began a very strange and (now) somewhat embarrassing episode that I have very rarely spoken of. The timing of it meant that I had no opportunity to prepare anybody or even to discuss it beforehand. So, all I could do was write notes to friends and neighbours explaining my decision and asking them to refrain from contacting me for the next forty days. The one person whom I excepted from this was Meegan, she and I would converse as usual, though I explained to her that until the retreat was over neither of us could have visits from friends.

The retreat began on 10 March 1991, with a mood of utter submission and openness to whatever would come; a mood born out of the belief that what would come was the final healing of the still open wound of Margaret Healy's death. What did come was something quite different.

By the end of the first week I had made resolutions to eat only raw, wholesome food; to delete the words I, me, my, and mine from my vocabulary; to give up the tenancy on my home and give away all material possessions; and to become God's instrument (!).

By the completion of the second week I (or rather, this being) had begun a rigorous fitness regime; was simultaneously undertaking the severe water-only fast described in

The Essene Gospel; and, was viewing myself as God's assistant.

By the completion of the third week the fast, which consisted of three days of utter agony followed by four days of bliss, had ended; the process of dispossession was well underway; and a sense of invincibility was now all-pervading.

By the mid-point of the retreat a distinct change had taken place in how I viewed both the world and myself. I felt enormously calm and unshakeably certain about everything. I'd developed a total acceptance of the view that, 'Life unfolds as it will.' There is no need to search for answers, for there are no questions. Life just is.

Then, on the 26th day of the retreat reality brutally intruded when I received a message from my mother saying that Steve was critically ill and was not expected to live beyond the next day or two. She asked that I break the retreat and come to the hospital to visit him.

Steve was thirty-nine. He had a wife, an eight-year-old son and a twenty-year-old step-daughter, all of whom he adored, a bright career ahead of him as a public relations officer in the public service, and he was a respected, long-serving member of Australia's renowned Surf Life Saving Association. He was deeply mourned by many people, not least by the close-knit group of friends with whom he had shared an amazing twenty-five-year journey since their days together at high school.

His early demise seemed all wrong, and in many ways that's true. Yet he faced his death with a quiet calmness and acceptance that some of those around him found difficult to emulate. This is not to imply that his dying was without sorrow, regret or difficulty – of which he felt plenty – but rather to indicate the manner in which he embraced his passing. In life, he was a colourful, popular character with a dry wit and a quick, wry humour. In dying, those qualities remained his allies to the end.

When I first arrived at his bedside in the Royal Perth Hospital he seemed anything but a dying man as he regaled me with a gleeful story about discovering that the man in the adjoining bed used to be our neighbour twenty years ago when we first moved to Perth. He described with some hilarity how it was our Aunt Wynne who'd recognized the man when she visited the ward. 'Eh up, Guiseppe,' said Wynne, in her still strong Manchester accent, 'what are you doing 'ere?' 'I'm a dyin',' he replied mournfully, in his still strong Italian accent.

It was to be a refrain that punctuated the air many times over the next six days and nights. Guiseppe wanted to have his family around him at all times, so if he awoke to find himself alone he would furiously press the nurses' buzzer, calling out, 'I'm a dyin'! I'm a dyin'! Getta the family! Getta the family!'

Dutifully, the family always came. Then, on the seventh morning, when Guiseppe's bed was empty, Steve, with dry mirth, recounted the story of Guiseppe's usual nocturnal demand not being met, which resulted in Guiseppe promptly dying.

The following night Steve had a most unusual occurrence; he awoke from sleep and felt himself to be completely free of the cancer. Swinging his legs out of bed (something it should have been impossible to achieve given that the cancer was in his spine), he announced to Mum, who was doing the night vigil, that he was cured. 'Get my clothes,' he said, 'I'm going home!' He stood up and started to take a step before Mum, who was frantically buzzing the nurses, took hold of him and guided him back into bed where he once again surrendered to his illness.

By now, over a week had passed since being told that Steve's death was imminent, yet in many ways he seemed to be getting stronger, at least in spirit. In part that was due to improved pain management, but it was also a common perception among visitors that he was nowhere near death's door. After this nocturnal episode, however, he definitely began a downward slide.

He still remained remarkably lucid, though because of the morphine his eyeballs began to float loose in their sockets making it difficult for him to focus visually, which had the effect of turning his attention inwards. This caused a marked shift in his own perception of why death was taking longer to come than was predicted, causing him to continually ask the same question over and over, 'What is it I'm supposed to be doing or saying or thinking before I can die? There must be something required of me, what is it?'

This question, though earnestly asked, wasn't causing him undue distress, at least not to my mind, but for his wife, Sue, and for Mum, it was both unbearable to hear and impossible to answer. In fact, by this time they were both feeling highly stressed and exhausted and were therefore sensitive to every little nuance that might indicate whether Steve was at the end of his tether.

To me, the situation looked quite different. Steve's questioning gave me hope that he was going to recognize something momentous about himself. Throughout this time we talked quite openly and freely about the path we had each taken in life; identifying the times and places where they had converged, and where they had parted. This was important to both of us because in the six months before his death we had been totally estranged from each other due to a family argument. Yet during these deathbed talks we came to a better understanding of each other than at any other time of our life.

Strangely though, he also became somebody other than my brother during this time; he became something of a universal representative of humankind. Talking with him and caring for him during the final days of his life gave me a strong sense of the inadequacy of seeing only the small, personal identity that the body portrays. He was so much more than the frail, bruised, degenerating body that lay before me; or, for that matter, than the strong, athletic, vigorous one that previously stood before me. He was now on the very threshold of crossing over from knowing himself only as Steve Connor to knowing himself as much, much more. This, I believe, is what his question was taking him towards. But before he had the chance to find the answer for himself he was thwarted by the actions of others.

Steve's question bothered Mum and Sue so much that, in order to find a solution, they asked a priest to visit Steve. As it happened, I was alone with Steve when the priest came; and graciously, he suggested that I should remain by the bedside while he talked with Steve. He explained to Steve that he'd spoken to Sue and Mum who had told him about the bothersome questions. He then placed his hand on Steve's forehead and very gently told him that there was no further need to worry himself about anything; there was no need to open his eyes, listen to anybody's voice, to think or question. All he had to do was let go. There was something so deeply relaxing and reassuring about his words, that Steve was soon in a deep sleep. The priest smiled at me and left.

I continued to sit by Steve's bed, watching him sleeping peacefully, unsure of how I felt about what had just taken place. There was definitely a certain logic to the advice of just letting go, of disconnecting from all that was happening around him; and of course the advice replicated the very consciousness I'd developed over the weeks of the retreat. Yet there was still so much life in Steve that the advice seemed premature. In fact, just the night before we'd witnessed how lively Steve's mind still was when his best friend Johnno, a television journalist, came for his usual evening visit after finishing work. John sat on Steve's bed, opened up a beer, and said, 'What a shit day I've had.' Quick as a flash, Steve replied, 'I'll swap with you.' John grimaced and hung his head in shame, but Steve just grinned at him, happy to have discovered that he could still outwit his sharpest mate.

An hour or so after the priest had left, Mum and Sue returned to the hospital. Steve was still sleeping so we went into the nearby waiting room while I told them what the priest had said. As we were talking, a nurse walking down the corridor glanced as usual through the window of Steve's room as she passed. Her face registered horrified shock as she swiftly opened the door and ran in, with the rest of us close behind. What we saw was Steve pulling himself up on the handle above the bed and swinging one leg over the edge, balanced precariously. His eyes were flashing wildly as he shouted, 'Get me out of this fucking place!'

I stood in the doorway transfixed as I watched the three women cajole him back into bed. He offered little resistance and was soon sleeping again. A few minutes after this, Wynne returned from a day out at the zoo with Meegan and Scott, Steve's son. Glad of the distraction, I took them down to the café for our evening meal, happy to hear their tales and their laughter. Both the children spent several hours each day at the hospital; they were a year apart in age and had become very close to each other. It was a great relief to all of us to see the way that they held close to each other during this difficult time.

While we were still eating dinner, Wynne came into the café to ask me to return upstairs to speak with Sue and Mum. I could see from the gravity of her expression that something was up, but exactly what it was came as a terrible shock. Mum and Sue told me that they had just had a meeting with Steve's consultant, who had agreed to their request for immediate euthanasia to be administered to Steve.

'No! You can't do that! He hasn't asked for it!' I spluttered, caught offguard.

'He's suffered enough. It has to end.'

'That's for him to decide, not you,' I argued.

'Anybody with an ounce of decency in them wouldn't let a dog suffer like this, let alone somebody they love.'

'You can't do it. It's not legal,' I countered.

'Well, it's been agreed. The priest will be here shortly to administer the last rites.'

'This is wrong! He's got several more days to live yet.'

'How can you possibly want this go on?' said Mum. 'Are you completely heartless? Anyway, it's not fair either to Steve or to Jayne to let this go on for another three days because then it means Jayne will have her birthday ruined again. I'm not going to allow that to happen and I know Steve would agree.'

'If you are so convinced this is the right thing, I dare you to go in there and ask him to agree to this!' My voice was now very loud, and though I knew my manner was becoming threatening, I didn't care. I wasn't going to back away.

'Some of us care about him so much we wouldn't dream of adding a single further burden upon him, whereas you've never cared about anybody but yourself. We're not going in there to talk to him about this, and neither are you.' Said Mum.

'If you go ahead with this, I won't go back into his room at all. I won't be a party to what you're proposing,' I threatened.

'Suit yourself, you usually do.'

We parted on very hostile terms, they unable to understand my 'hard-heartedness', me unable to understand their complicity. I returned to the café and spoke only two words to Wynne, 'It's wrong.' We then all sat in silence until the appointed time of the 'lethal dose' and the last rites was upon us. We arrived back at the ward just as the summoned inner circle of Steve's closest friends and Sue's relatives were gathering to witness Steve's passing. It made me feel sick to see that so many people were willing to condone his premature death. I wanted to call out and make a scene; to dare each one of them to ask Steve's permission for this deed to be done, but I didn't. Nor did I go to him myself and tell him what was going to be done to him; instead I simply sat quietly in the corridor feeling powerless to do anything other than to let the events unfold as they must.

The first person to come out of the room was the priest, the same one whom I had met earlier in the day. He sat beside me and asked how I was doing.

'What's happened in there was wrong. Steve has never, ever, spoken of euthanasia.' I defiantly declared.

He nodded his head slightly, leaned forward in his chair, looked at his hands for a few moments, and then said, 'Steve won't die tonight.'

'But he's been given a fatal overdose, hasn't he?'

'He won't succumb. I've seen this before. I don't know how long he can hold out, but he won't die tonight. He's not ready yet; and, he's a fighter.'

'Well if you believe that why did you participate?' I asked, incredulously.

'It's my observation that the way a person dies is a direct reflection of the way they have lived. The dynamic that has been played out here between your mother, your sister-in-law, and Steve, is doubtless consistent with the way Steve has always related to them, and they to him. It's not my place to interfere with the final act of that drama.'

The obvious truth of what he was saying struck home immediately, but at the time it didn't help to alleviate the pain and anger that was coursing through me. Instead, I continued to sit in the corridor casting surly looks and feeling wretched. Then, after an hour or so, one or two people left Steve's room to go outside for a smoke, ruefully noting that he hadn't succumbed yet. A little while later, more people came out into the corridor looking clearly agitated that, 'it was taking so long'.

One of Steve's friends came to sit beside me, shaking his head in wry bemusement as he described the sombre mood that was present in the room during the administering of the Last Rites. A mood that was abruptly shattered when Steve awoke, squinted his best eye to get a better look at the proceedings, and then said, 'Is that you again Father? Gee, things must be really serious this time.'

Reportedly, unconsciousness quickly overtook him again, allowing those present some scope for regaining their composure. However, over the next few hours, whenever there was an expectant hush that he was about to take his last breath, he would suddenly let rip with a string of gibberish about surf-boat racing. 'Why won't the stubborn bugger just die?' his friend lamented.

By 10 pm, four hours after the Last Rites, most of those

present had given up and gone home. Only Steve's wife and her sister remained in the room, with me still keeping watch from the corridor. By 2 am I'd begun to believe that Steve actually was going to foil this plan, so I too went home. When I returned at 9 am the following morning, Meegan, who had stayed the night at Mum's, was in the hospital lobby to greet me. It was she who broke the news to me that Steve had died an hour earlier.

His body lay in the same bed, albeit now freshly made with crisp sheets. The plethora of medical equipment that had surrounded him and pierced him was gone. The room, you might say, was 'deathly still'. The yellow, waxy, mask-like face with its slack jaw and open mouth was certainly reminiscent of Steve, yet to look upon this face was to look upon something unknown. I left the room knowing that it wasn't Steve who was about to be collected by the undertaker; it was only his corpse. Steve was already somewhere else.

His death occurred on the 38th day of my 'retreat'. On the 41st day, the day that I had envisaged heralding a new dawn for me, Steve's funeral was held. The crematorium chapel was filled to capacity with mourners wanting to pay their last respects; the eulogies were funny yet respectful, and their loss, though keenly felt, didn't eclipse their feelings of warm reverence for a life well lived. As for the euthanasia issue, well, it just became another part of our family history that never gets talked about.

January 1991

8

1991–2003

After the funeral, I had to start facing the consequences of the retreat. Meegan and I were homeless, devoid of possessions, in mourning, and temporarily lodged in a cheap hotel room in Fremantle, Perth. It could so easily have been over-whelmingly demoralizing, but instead there was a sort of surreal liberation to it. I no longer saw myself as God's assistant, but I did now see undeniable evidence that the events of my life were not randomly thrown together.

It could not have been mere coincidence that my thoughts about the retreat just happened to come *exactly* forty days before the anniversary of the accident. It could not have been mere coincidence that my family was once again facing a death trauma *exactly* twenty years after the previous time. Clearly, something other than chance was at work here, and though I didn't know what or who, I found comfort in just knowing that it was so. I felt sure that no harm would come to either Meegan or myself if I could remain alert to what it was that was being asked of me. I was quite certain that nothing was being imposed but rather something very valuable was being offered. All I had to do was recognize and accept it.

Mind you, that didn't mean I could withdraw again from the world and contemplate my navel while waiting for the revelation to descend from on high. What the retreat had taught me was to look and listen for spiritual revelation from both within and without. Every person, every event, every thought, every feeling could potentially contain an essential message. Then again, it might not. The task now was to discern which was which.

The first decision I made was that we should remain in Fremantle so that Meegan could continue at the Steiner school. However, the urge to dispossess had been so strong during the retreat that I knew it still had to be honoured. So when, by a stroke of good fortune, I stumbled across a notice for long-term accommodation at the Fremantle YHA, a hostel for travellers, it seemed the perfect solution, and so it proved to be.

The YHA building was another rather large, squat rectangle, much like Bay Apartments where I'd lived almost twenty years before. My heart sank a little when I saw the size of it, until discovering that the long-term accommodation was set in its own small, discrete corner of the building. There were seven rooms; two singles, four doubles, and one family size, which at the time was occupied by another single mother with two children – hence Meegan and I moved into a double room. The occupants, maximum fourteen, shared a large bathroom, a smallish lounge room, and a tiny kitchen. It was lovely; we stayed for a year and had rarely been happier.

This time also marked a deepening of my interest in the philosophy that stands behind the work of Rudolf Steiner, which he named anthroposophy. I'd been attending lectures at the school and reading some of Steiner's books, but I was still deeply bothered by the Christian influence. Especially so, since discovering that a church called the Christian Community, which was handing out leaflets at the school fair, was part of the anthroposophical impulse. I was complaining about this 'infiltration' to another of the parents in Meegan's class, saying that I wished it were possible to have a secular

Steiner school, when she said, 'There is one, it's in New South Wales.' My heart leapt; this was it! This was the message I'd been waiting for!

Moreover, the timing couldn't have been more perfect. It had only been a few days prior to this that the YHA had announced an intention to sell the Fremantle building so we would have to move anyway. And it assuaged the recent disappointment of being rejected for a visa to study anthroposophy in America due to insufficient income. American officialdom took exception to the notion that a person whose only income is single parent benefit could possibly manage to budget for anything as unnecessary as study and travel. Nor were they impressed when I pointed out that the exchange rate conversion would actually give me a higher income than American single mothers were expected to survive on.

I could understand their concern though: after all, even I didn't understand how I was able to make my money stretch. It helped that I didn't smoke, drink, drive a car, or socialize much, but nevertheless we lived a very good life considering that my income was officially below the poverty line. We dressed well, always in natural fabrics of cotton, linen, wool and silk, almost all of which were purchased at charity shops. It constantly amazed me what lovely quality clothes people gave away, many of which seemed to be almost new.

I never felt deprived, quite the opposite: I felt enormously privileged to be able to live a life freed from the constraints of career, mortgage, debts, and social aspiration. It allowed me to take up options that others might not even be aware of like the privilege of doing voluntary work for the Peace and Environment movement; and it allowed me to value the small things that I might otherwise have ignored. One such special little ritual which developed between Meegan and myself was to dress up in some costume finery that we'd discovered in a charity shop, then go to a posh restaurant and order just one dessert that we'd then share. Our other favourite 'treat' was to sit on the beach at sunset sharing fish and chips.

When the prospect of crossing the continent was once again presented to me, therefore, it didn't occur to me to wonder about the cost, only about whether it was the right thing for us to do. Fortunately, Meegan was as keen as I was, so 18 months after Steve's death we were on the move again. This time to a small town in NSW.

I always love arriving in a new place. I loved experiencing the new sights, sounds and smells and seeing new characteristics in the people, the buildings, and the environment; but most especially I loved the excitement of not knowing what's waiting for me. I loved this excitement because almost always there's something positive, something completely unimagined, and something wondrous about meeting the new.

This time my excitement was especially high. I was about to meet the very embodiment of a wish I'd held for the past seven years: a Steiner school that embraces all the best qualities of the curriculum and the philosophy, but leaves aside what I considered then the outdated, unnecessary, and irritating Christian influence. What a relief it was going to be. What a joy it would be to encounter other people who obviously had reached the same conclusions as me. People who had the same ability to recognize that a spiritual outlook didn't have to be a Christian outlook. What a shame it was that brilliant Dr Steiner had failed to free himself from the clutches of the Church. Still, never mind, it was happening now, that's all that mattered.

It was with such thoughts and high hopes that I embraced

life at this new place. The town itself was rather sweet and quaint, with the shop frontages on the single main street retaining much of their original, late nineteenth century condition. The school itself was situated quite a long way out of town, which necessitated a 40-minute bus ride twice a day along a winding road that traversed an exquisite rainforest. But beautiful as the scenery was along the way it was a mere appetizer for the gorgeous setting of the school, which was nestled deep in a lush rainforest valley. The wood and glass classrooms, wrapped around by sweeping wooden verandas, merged into the surrounding foliage in a way that made them look as though they'd always been there. It was breathtakingly lovely.

Why then, I had to wonder, did the children seem so unusually aggressive? Three separate scuffles broke out in just the couple of hours that I was there for the enrolment process. What was even more surprising was the lack of response these scuffles got from the several teachers who witnessed them; they all seemed quite unconcerned, even though the encounters were far from the usual push and shove that one might expect amongst children. I tried to ignore the little warning bell that had started tinkling, but by the end of the first week it was clanking constantly.

Meegan's class was preparing to give a drama performance at a local festival, so she was given a part, along with a script from which she had to rehearse at home. Plays are an intrinsic part of life in Waldorf schools, so this was a routine we were well used to. However, when I saw the state of the script I was appalled. It appeared to have been prepared by someone who had no skill in typing, grammar, spelling or punctuation. It was such a terrible mess that I could hardly bring myself to read it, let alone condone Meegan reading it as homework.

At the performance a week later, I broached the subject of the script with the class teacher, saying that although I appreciated the effort of whoever had typed the script, it surely wasn't appropriate to give such a shoddy piece of work to the students. After all, I said, you wouldn't want them to think this level of work was acceptable, would you? She looked at me for a moment before saying, 'I typed it, and yes I think it's quite acceptable. I don't aspire to perfection.' The clanging of the bell was so loud I was quite unable to formulate a reply.

The final straw came just a few days later when Meegan arrived home from school with a very badly lacerated knee caused from tripping over while running downhill to catch the bus. The fact that no one even noticed the accident, let alone that a badly injured child could board the bus unobserved, and then make the long journey home without anyone offering comfort, was more than I could tolerate. Meegan was the most sure-footed of children; she climbed and frolicked like a tomboy and had never before had an injury anything like this. To my mind this confirmed that something was clearly going terribly wrong.

When her wound had begun to heal I asked if she would be willing to let me home-school her for a while, and she accepted without hesitation. Initially, this worked really well. I'd learnt enough about the Steiner curriculum to be able to knock together a pretty good facsimile of it. We'd spend the morning 'in class' and then have some kind of activity in the afternoon; but after a couple of weeks, we both knew it wasn't going to work long term. Once I'd admitted that to myself, a blanket of despair began to descend. I felt utterly bereft of ideas or direction, and totally distrustful of my ability to make worthwhile decisions.

It was while in this mood, hunched in a chair, feeling deeply sorry for myself, that I finally asked myself the question, 'What's the point to all this?' From the right-hand side, slightly above me, came a strong male voice declaring, 'The purpose of anthroposophy is to lead people to the Christ.' I jumped out of my seat. Nobody was there, all was quiet. Yet the phrase was seared into me: 'The purpose of anthroposophy is to lead people to the Christ.' In a split second everything became clear. The problems we were encountering were simply the means to bring me to this point.

Without hesitating a second, or even giving it any conscious thought, I knew what had to be done next. I had to contact a priest of the Christian Community and find out where I could study an anthroposophical understanding of Christianity. I immediately tracked down the name and address of a priest in Sydney, and wrote a letter explaining what I wanted to do. When his reply hadn't arrived a week later, I phoned him to ask where I could undertake such a study.

'Do you want to be a priest?' he asked.

'No, I just want to have an anthroposophical understanding of Christianity.'

'The seminary is probably the only place you can do that, but it's in Stuttgart. Are you prepared to go to Germany?'

'Yes, but do they teach in English?'

'No, only German.'

'Well, I don't speak German, so you will just have to be my teacher instead.'

'I can't do that [laughing].'

'Why not? You've studied there haven't you?'

'Yes, but...'

'Well, I'm sorry to be pushy but this is obviously the way it has to be. When can I meet with you?'

He only agreed to meet with me once he'd realized that I was a twelve-hour train ride away from Sydney. He assumed, wrongly, that the distance meant I wouldn't follow through with my intention. A week later, on 29 September 1992, Meegan and I arrived in Sydney. We spent the next day celebrating her eleventh birthday; then, on 1 October I was sitting opposite the priest, Martin Samson, telling him my life story, and feeling, for the first time ever, that I'd met somebody who not only accepted what I was saying, but who could actually understand it. Two hours later I left having extracted a promise from Martin that he would be my teacher if I moved to Sydney. He also extracted a promise from me that I would complement my study by regularly attending the sacramental life of the church, even if it was only so that I could offer some proper criticism of it.

Two months later we were living in Sydney. Meegan was back at a Steiner school and I was engaged in vigorous theological discussions with Martin. I was also, much to my surprise, quietly accepting the sacramental rituals that accompanied my studies. The sombre, contemplative mood of the communion service, the 'Act of Consecration of Man', felt like a deeply healing space in which I could allow myself to simply be a still and silent observer. Perhaps there were momentous events taking place at the altar, perhaps not, but whichever view I or any other member of the congregation held, it remained entirely private. The service provided absolutely no opportunity for anybody to proclaim their faith, demonstrate their piety, or surrender their will. It seemed to me an utterly amazing achievement in contradiction; a religious service that left people completely free, completely private.

The other way in which this contradiction worked magnificently was Bible study, an activity that previously would have brought out the screaming banshee in me. However, in the Christian Community, instead of interpreting a biblical passage, one simply but rigorously observes whatever the author has presented. For instance: Who are the people, have they met before, is the scene depicting action or dialogue, is the language using past or present or future tense, etc. Initially I found it incredibly difficult to differentiate between observation and interpretation, but as that distinction developed so too did my ability to see the poetic skill and artistry of the biblical writers – which, in quite unexpected ways, then opens up entirely new dimensions within this ancient text.

It was a process that was also opening up new dimensions within me. Martin's willingness to share what he knew about the cosmic dimensions of life fuelled my own need to know more about the cosmic experiences I'd had. To do that meant getting to know a lot more about Rudolf Steiner and his teachings. So, alongside my studies with Martin, I enrolled as a full-time student at Parsifal College, Sydney, to study for a Certificate in Anthroposophical Studies.

The year 1993, my year at Parsifal, would rank alongside 1981 (Meegan's birth) and 1971 (Margaret Healy's death), as a powerful turning point in my life. It felt as if everything that had gone before had happened for the express purpose of leading me towards this moment. The sheer joy and relief of dedicating day after day to the task of learning about the interplay of the spiritual world with the material world was like being given a daily dose of manna. We studied such subjects as the Evolution of Human Consciousness, The

Human Being and Cosmology, Female/Male Studies, Karma and Reincarnation, and Science and Phenomenology — all complemented by classes in painting, sculpture, speech and drama, weaving, and creative writing.

Not that it was all sweetness and light, far from it, there were all the personality clashes and disharmony that afflicts any group of people, not to mention the natural resistance we often feel when encountering something new. There was the occasion, for instance, when I furiously denounced the notion that to love a murderer could be noble. This situation occurred during a creative writing class while being told about a man who, when liberated from a concentration camp after the war, was found to be in remarkably better health than his fellow Jews even though he had suffered the same enormous deprivation. This man had allegedly witnessed Nazi soldiers cold-bloodedly shooting his wife and children at close range, but he was spared death and taken to a concentration camp because his translation skills were needed.

Once at the camp, he was treated with special brutality because it was expected that he would feel particularly aggrieved towards his captors. Yet, according to the story, the opposite happened. The man began to realize that only loveless, unloved beings could commit the kind of atrocities that the Nazis were committing. So he resolved to stop thinking of them as barbaric murderers and instead to feel love for them. The more love he felt for them, the stronger and more healthy he became.

When this story ended, most of my fellow students were misty-eyed and gooey, but I was enraged. 'This man betrayed his family's honour!' I bellowed at the lecturer, 'How can you describe him as a hero; he's a coward and a traitor!' He didn't attempt to dissuade me, nor did he feel the need to defend his position, he just let me rage on. When I was done, he nodded his head sagely, rubbed his chin, thanked me for putting another perspective, and then calmly suggested that we begin our writing exercise – a story about an unwitting benefactor.

Over the ensuing ten years, I've thought long and hard about this Jewish man, looking at his story from every angle. The pivotal question of whether it really was possible to love one's enemy in such a wholehearted way frequently exercised my mind. What it took me a long time to realize is that the story was asking me whether I was ready to forgive and to be forgiven.

There were many gifts and blessings resulting from Parsifal College, including particularly cherished friendships. However, one of the most important moments of the entire year very nearly passed me by unnoticed. We were studying Steiner's book, *Knowledge of the Higher Worlds*, one of the five foundational books of anthroposophy, for which I was meant to prepare a presentation of Chapter III. But when the day came I hadn't even read the chapter, let alone prepared a response. Hence, I had to just own up to my failing and offer to read the chapter aloud instead. In theory, this should have made the exercise easier, but in reality it turned out to be an exquisitely excruciating experience of self-discovery.

I unexpectedly found myself reading words that described my life, that explained my life, that gave me the clearest understanding so far of what had happened to me and why. Both my mind and my heart were racing with equal degrees of excitement and apprehension. Yet all the while that I was reading, I knew that I had to calmly maintain a neutral demeanour; I had to pretend that the words meant nothing personal to me. I had to keep my discovery to myself and let it lie quietly, ever so quietly, however long it took for the day to arise when I could say, yes, these words apply to me.

The chapter, entitled Initiation, describes the obstacles that will beset the path of the modern candidate for spiritual initiation; an initiation which, unlike in the old days of the secret mystery temples, is now undertaken while living an ordinary, everyday existence. The obstacles, which are known as trials, are designed to ensure that the candidate has attained the necessary degree of maturity to be able to rightly receive 'the secrets of existence'. The first of these trials is known as the *Fire-Trial* because its intention is to burn away all the superfluous dross of life that prevents us from seeing the higher aspects of nature, of others, and of the self.

Steiner says:

> For many people, ordinary life is itself a more or less unconscious process of initiation through the Fire-Trial. Such people have passed through a wealth of experience, so that their self-confidence, courage and fortitude have been greatly strengthened in a normal manner while learning to bear sorrow, disappointment and failure in their undertakings with greatness of soul, and especially with equanimity and unbroken strength. Thus they are often initiates without knowing it, and it then needs but little to unseal their spiritual hearing and sight so that they become clairvoyant.* For it must be noted that a genuine fire-trial is not intended to satisfy the curiosity of the candidate. It is true that s/he learns many uncommon things of

---

*When Steiner uses the word clairvoyant he means the ability to consciously perceive spiritual beings and spiritual intention; *not* to read tea leaves and tell fortunes.

which others can have no inkling, but this acquisition of knowledge is not the end, but the means to the end; the end consists in the attainment, thanks to this knowledge of the higher worlds, of greater and truer self-confidence, a higher degree of courage, and a magnanimity and perseverance such as cannot, as a rule, be acquired in the lower world.

The candidate may always turn back after the fire-trial. S/he will then resume life, strengthened in body and soul, and wait for a future incarnation to continue initiation. In the present incarnation s/he will prove a more useful member of society and of humanity than before. In whatever position one may find oneself, firmness, prudence, resoluteness, and a beneficent influence over one's fellows will have greatly increased.*

However, if the candidate for initiation should wish to continue the path, a second trial, the *Water-Trial,* awaits. This involves developing the ability to 'decipher the occurrences and the beings of the spiritual world like the characters of a text.' In other words, all facets of life can reveal their part in the cosmic script once we know the language of the script. The candidate for the second trial must learn this language, and in doing so further aspects of higher existence will become known.

Thanks to this language the student also learns certain rules of conduct and certain duties of which s/he formerly knew nothing. Having learned these s/he is able to perform actions endowed with a significance and a meaning such as the actions of one not initiated can never possess. S/he acts

---

* *Knowledge of the Higher Worlds, How it is Achieved* (Rudolf Steiner Press, 1969). (Also, all following quotes.)

out of the higher worlds. Instructions concerning such action can only be read and understood in the writing in question.

Yet it must be emphasized that there are people unconsciously gifted with the ability and faculty of performing such actions, though they have never undergone an esoteric training. Such helpers of the world and of humanity pass through life bestowing blessings and performing good deeds. For reasons here not to be discussed, gifts have been bestowed on them that appear supernatural. What distinguishes them from the candidate for initiation is only that the latter acts consciously and with full insight into the entire situation. S/he acquires by training the gifts bestowed on others by higher powers for the good of humanity. We can sincerely revere these favoured of God; but we should not for this reason regard the work of esoteric training as superfluous.

Once the language of the cosmic script is learnt, the candidate will experience a marked shift. A definite task will be asked of the candidate, but there will be no outer reason to impel one either to undertake the task or to complete it. All the reason, all the impulse must come only from the candidate's ability to read the script. This trial is known as the *Water-Trial* because there is absolutely nothing solid under one's feet.

One human quality is of very special importance at this stage of initiation, namely, an *unquestionably sound judgement*. Attention should be paid to the training of this faculty during all the previous stages; for it now remains to be proved whether the candidate is shaping in a way that shows the student to be fit for the true path of knowledge. Further progress is now only possible if s/he is able to distinguish illusion, superstition, and everything fantastic, from true reality. This is, at first, more difficult to accomplish in the higher stages of existence than in the lower. Every prejudice, every cherished opinion with regard to the things in question, must vanish; truth alone must guide. There must be perfect readiness to abandon at once any idea, opinion, or inclination when logical thought demands it. Certainty in higher worlds is only likely to be attained when personal opinion is never considered.

People whose mode of thought tends to fancifulness and superstition can never make progress on the path to higher knowledge... Yet no one needs to believe that the student loses all sense of poetry in life, all power of enthusiasm because the words: *You must be rid of all prejudice* are written over the portal leading to the second trial of initiation, and because over the portal at the entrance to the first trial s/he reads: *Without normal common sense all thine efforts are in vain.*

Once the *Fire-Trial* and the *Water-Trial* have been successfully completed, a third trial awaits those who choose not to turn back. This time there is no definite goal to be reached, there is no cosmic script to follow, and there is nothing and nobody to turn to for strength. This is where the candidate requires the ability to rely on the self, and to find the way to come to rapid decisions that are based on spiritual inspiration.

There is no time for doubt or hesitation. Every moment of hesitation would prove that s/he was still unfit. Whatever prevents the candidate from listening to the voice of the spirit must be courageously overcome. It is a question of showing presence of mind in this situation, and the training at this stage is concerned with the perfect development of this quality. All the accustomed inducements to act or even to think now cease. In order not to remain inactive one must not lose the self, for only within oneself can one find the central point of vantage where one can gain a firm hold. No one on reading this, without further acquaintance with these matters, should feel an antipathy for this principle of being thrown back on oneself, for success in this trial brings with it a moment of supreme happiness.

Each one of these trials takes place in the course of ordinary, everyday existence. The candidate for modern initiation must not fail to recognize that meeting the challenges and problems of life is itself an initiation training.

A person who is quick to act when a misfortune is imminent, whereas a few moments of hesitation would have seen the misfortune an accomplished fact, and who has turned this ability into a permanent personal quality, has unconsciously acquired the degree of maturity necessary for the third trial. For at this stage everything centres round the development of absolute presence of mind. This trial is known as the *Air-Trial,* because while undergoing it one can support oneself neither upon the firm basis of external incentive nor upon the figures, tones, and colours that one has learned at the stages of *preparation* and *enlightenment,* but exclusively upon oneself.

Reading these words aloud to my colleagues was really quite terrifying. Each new sentence made me feel further exposed. I knew that the words applied to me but I didn't want anybody else to know because the concept of being thought of as a candidate for initiation was too shockingly alien to contemplate. What did it mean to be an initiate? What would be expected of me? How was it possible to be an initiate but not know about it? If I really was an initiate why hadn't somebody noticed it by now?

These were the questions that surfaced during the course of the reading; and, though I could have sought advice from my tutors, or from Martin, I didn't. Instead, the lesson that I had learnt all those years ago about keeping silent kicked in. Which is just as well really because they were the wrong questions. Or, at least, the intention behind the questions was wrong because it was founded on the assumption that initiation was something extraordinary, something special, something that set one apart from, and above, the rest of humanity. Which means I was relating to the old form of initiation, the one that has fallen into decadence. The kind of initiation Steiner is referring to is quite different as should have been plain to me from his description of the *Trials*.

Yet it took several more years of silent observation and deep personal reflection before I was able to take a more detached look at why the chapter on the *Trials* had affected me so deeply. The answer, which you might have already guessed, is that I had immediately connected what I was reading with what I'd experienced all those years ago during the nightly trials. Steiner's description of the *Trials* so closely matched the demands of the angels, it was natural for me to presume that because I had directly experienced the working of the beings that stand behind the *Trials*, I must therefore be an initiate.

I now know that's not true; I'm not an initiate, at least not in the sense that I can converse with spirit beings at will. I am in an initiation process, though; a process that asks me to become ever more awake to spiritual input and existence. Every person on earth is participating in the *Trials* in one way or another. If each one of us were to lay out a map of the biographical journey we've traversed, the evidence would be clear to see. Perhaps, though, one of the reasons we are not inclined to do this is that the *Trials* by their very nature are intimately bound up with the difficulties of life.

Yet it's through the *Trials* of my biography that it became my destiny to gain a glimpse of the spiritual beings who act both as our mentors and as our adversaries during this initiation process, though at present I do not know the reason why that privilege should have fallen to me. Perhaps it was simply so that I could write this book to offer confirmation to any who may want to receive it that we are, each one of us, part of a wondrous process of spiritual artistry. I now see each individual and each unique biographical path as a work of art, one in which both the individual and the spiritual worlds have equal creative input — even during, perhaps especially during, times of great upheaval.

We are 'works in progress'. We are delicate, yet malleable pieces of art whose shape and colour continually show new texture, new lustre, and infinitely new possibilities. It's as if the events that we meet in life represent one hand of the spiritual artist, while the way we individually meet each event represents the work of the other hand. Thus each life is continuously shaped and moulded. Thus we are freed from the cold hand of rigidity.

Yet as significant and wondrous as these discoveries are, perhaps the most important aspect of my exploration of the insights of Rudolf Steiner has been the understanding he provides about life after death. Thanks to Rudolf Steiner I now know that the beings whom I met during the evening trials are the very beings we will all meet upon crossing the threshold of death. They are the keepers of destiny, the keepers of 'karma'. It is their task to ensure that each of us meet, with as much consciousness as possible, the effect and consequence of our life on earth, in order that we each know what steps we have taken in our initiation process.

It is common knowledge that people who've had a near-death experience see a panorama of their life unfolding at the moment of death. However, according to Steiner, this flash panorama is only the starting point of a considerable process through which each of us will pass in order to review the life that has just ended. He describes a second panoramic vista occurring for the three days that immediately follow death, beginning at the moment of death and proceeding in reverse order to the moment of birth, giving the departing person a comprehensive view of the life that has been lived.

For most of us this will be a decidedly unpleasant experience given that we modern humans have devised ingenious ways of neglecting to see, or to remember, many of the mistakes and failures of our life. However, this three-day vista is only a prelude to the main event, an experience that Steiner calls 'kamaloca'. When we enter kamaloca many things happen, but my focus will be on only three of them. The first is a sense of being under intense scrutiny, of having nowhere to hide, of being completely exposed and vulnerable. The very human trait of concealing one's thoughts and feelings (often even to oneself) is no longer possible. All the barriers are down; all the games are over.

Simultaneously, all the longings and desires for what has been left behind – people, possessions, body, identity, food, substances, sex, money, influence etc. – come flooding to the fore, causing extreme anguish. Kamaloca offers no respite, no distractions, no compromises. Each of us must experience the intensity of our loss in order to understand the extent of our descent into materialism. In other words, the extent of our disconnection from the spiritual. There is no malice intended in this suffering; on the contrary, it is simply a natural consequence of the evolutionary path of consciousness.

Then, the third, deeply significant, aspect of kamaloca begins to unfold, the third phase of the panoramic vistas experienced earlier. However, this time a most important new dimension enters; the emphasis is no longer on what the self experienced, but rather on how others experienced you. Think about this for a moment. How would it be to receive a totally uncensored account and direct experience of the effect you have had on *all* the people you've ever encountered? *All* the events you've ever participated in, the hearts you've broken, the loyalties you've betrayed, the anger you've expressed. And, thankfully, the love, kindness, joys and compassion you've freely given to others.

The unfolding of the third vista again occurs in reverse order, beginning at death, ending at birth. It continues for a time approximate to one third of the time alive, so that if one dies at age 60, kamaloca would last for around twenty years. What an unbearable ordeal, you might be thinking. Well, yes, definitely, and yet, no, not really. The yes aspect is the severe reality of having the truth of our behaviour starkly exposed; the no aspect is the opportunity this gives us to find compassion for another, and, as a consequence to find the resolve to put our wrongs right.

It is during kamaloca that we uncover the aspects of ourselves that need to continue the journey of evolution. It is here that we recognize which of our behaviours caused so much pain to others that we must make amends for them. It is here that we find whether we have achieved any of the karmic intentions we brought with us to earth, and again realize our true nature, our true purpose. It is here that we sort the dross from the gold and, most importantly, that we again understand our part in the manifold workings of the spiritual realms and of the continual interaction between the earthly realm and its spiritual counterpart. To put it in more concrete terms, the kamaloca period offers the possibility of keeping open a degree of connection between the living and the dead.

This can be experienced quite distinctly for anybody who may want to assist the process of a loved one engaged in crossing the threshold. Or it can also be helpful initially to take a more detached perspective by simply observing where and when issues arise concerning those who have died. Many times I have had the experience of being in conversation and suddenly finding the topic turning to somebody who has died. At an appropriate moment, I'll ask for details about the age of the person and when they died; this then allows me to mentally calculate where that person is in terms of their kamaloca journey. (For instance, if the conversation is taking place in 2003 about a person who died in 2000 at age 50, then the three year real time gap translates into nine years of kamaloca, which means the person is now revisiting their 41st year, approximately).

Then I'll ask an open-ended question about what memories might be connected with the person at the age they are now revisiting in kamaloca (What was John/Mary doing at 41?). Invariably, the result is to find myself listening as a lament or regret comes tumbling forth. This has happened so many times that I have no doubt whatsoever that we, the living, are on some level part of the kamaloca journey of the dead. We sense, and in a certain way also re-live, the events that are being played out in kamaloca.

This might take many forms, but here are a few illustrations. A woman in her 50s was feeling an unusual need to speak to her mother who had died some ten years earlier. This need grew to such alarming proportions that the woman became uncharacteristically weepy. When I calculated the mother's kamaloca age and the daughter's corresponding age at the time, she was immediately able to identify a difficult situation that had passed between them. After being given the space to talk it through she was able, of her own volition, to express both compassion and forgiveness towards her mother, which allowed her to let go of the incident.

Another person, unable to contain the hurt and bitterness that she felt towards a deceased relative, began to talk with great agitation about an occasion on which she felt a deep humiliation had been perpetrated against her. My calculations revealed that the deceased person was at the kamaloca age of the event in question, though so deep was the hurt that no forgiveness or understanding was expressed.

Initially, I wasn't sure why such events occurred, but as my understanding of karma has deepened, so has the mystery begun to unravel. The spiritual intention behind kamaloca is to provide irrefutable proof of the importance of consequence, in particular the consequence of how we treat each other. Every action, every thought, every intention that we experience with or towards another person, binds us to that person *if* the other person holds onto it. In kamaloca we must endure the full pain of knowing exactly how much the other person is bound to the consequence of our previous encounters. The pain of this is amplified by the knowledge that once dead, we can no longer take steps to heal or rectify the situation.

And yet, each of us that are alive can still have influence over the way in which we allow consequence to remain bound up between the so-called dead and ourselves. We can choose to hold onto our thoughts and feelings towards the dead, or we can strive to loosen the bonds. After all, it is because we are bound together that our attention is called towards the kamaloca journey of the 'dead' one. In other words, after the threshold of death has been crossed, the dead are completely reliant on the living to effect any change in whatever karma (i.e. consequence) binds the two together.

It is by compassionate privilege that the living person has an opportunity to alter the consequence of the encounter. This is when we, the living, can strive to forgive past hurts and injustices. The extent of our success, or not, in this striving, determines the extent to which the consequences continue to be felt in kamaloca. Where there is no forgiveness to mitigate, the ties that bind and constrict must inevitably continue, which means both parties will sustain this ill will through as many incarnations as it takes until forgiveness reigns. This cycle will continue until we have the ability to look upon ourselves with unwavering honesty, and to look upon others with unwavering compassion.

For me, these indications of the workings of kamaloca provide great comfort and solace; yet I don't deny they also have strong elements of foreboding and dread. Does that sound paradoxical? Good, because the existence of paradox has become the first signpost I look for when assessing whether I'm on the right road to spiritual awareness. If it's not there, if everything is clear, precise, and free of complexity, then the path seems dubious, for the human condition is nothing if not perplexing.

However, my main reason for taking some comfort from kamaloca, derives from the small experience of it I had during the encounter with the angels and demons. Why is this comforting? Well, primarily because I now know that we don't have to suffer the consequences of our actions alone. The resolute commitment and allegiance of the angelic realm towards humanity is beyond my capabilities to describe, yet the knowledge of it burns so strongly within me that the fear of what I will meet in kamaloca is much abated. As for the demons, well, the role they play is considerable and formidable, yet it is very much dictated by the extent to which each of us relinquishes personal responsibility to them. The purpose of the demons is to distract our attention away from the higher purpose of life – the evolution of consciousness. This is a task made immeasurably easier for them by the kind of collective denial of spiritual reality that today prevents informed debate on spiritual matters taking place in western societies.

However, I take comfort from knowing that at the conclusion of kamaloca I will have a better idea of knowing where I have, unwittingly or not, colluded with the demons, and a clearer understanding of what I need to do to continue the quest of becoming more aware. After this begins the unimaginably intricate task of collaborating with the angelic realms in preparing the script for our next life. Such questions as: where to be born, to whom, into what race, culture, class, religion; with which gender and with what attributes and/or handicaps, etc., etc.

After the physical criteria are established, then come questions about which individuals we need to encounter, under which circumstances, with what intention? Then, what events and challenges does one need to encounter, what obstacles does one need to overcome? And of course, the only way to prepare this properly is to work in the spiritual realms with those whom we will need to encounter during our next incarnation. Together we write, plan, and even rehearse the way, the how, the when, and the where of our meetings. No wonder Steiner says we only incarnate roughly every 1,000 years! What a mammoth production, and what marvellous insight it provides into where the impulse for drama comes from. No wonder we are in thrall to Hollywood, and to playwrights and novelists for they, however unconsciously, are reminding us of a process that we have all undertaken before coming to earth. As Shakespeare wrote: *All the world's a stage, And all the men and women merely players.*

The idea of a cosmic script may sound repellent; after all, in one fell swoop it removes our cherished notion of being free to determine our own lives. At the same time it destroys any credibility we might have when it comes to blaming others for our misfortunes. Well, again, yes and no; welcome to paradox. This script does not in any way fix us in a pre-determined role but serves only to provide an outline of the required plot, characters, scenes and attire that will best assist the path of our evolution, an outline we have ourselves helped to design and construct. The full characterizations and the plot twists occur in the years between birth and death, sometimes at our own design, sometimes at the hand of others.

So, was the violent death of Margaret Healy part of my pre-birth intention? All the outer indications say yes. Circumstantially, the evidence does seem to validate the view that it was meant to happen. Is that possible? Is it conceivable that the angels would collude in a script that required one person to violently kill another? Every part of me says no. And yet...

And yet it does appear to be so.

Why? The specific answer, if there is one, is unavailable to me, though doubtless it will be revealed in kamaloca. Meanwhile, the only rationale with which I can attempt to traverse this moral morass is to apply the principles of karmic research and ask: What might I have to learn from this? What might be trying to work itself out here?

Clearly, my incarnation in this lifetime is completely dominated by the need to formulate a personal understanding of the moral cost of killing another person; a need highlighted by circumstances which prevented me from taking refuge in the bosom of family warmth, in an impersonal, objective punishment meted by the courts, in the considered rationale of medicine, or in the sanctity of the church. To write such a script for oneself would seem masochistic at best, or outright perversity at worst. At least, that's how it might seem when viewed through the lens of modern abstraction.

The lens I use asks me to walk the tightrope of distinguishing between something having to happen karmically, and something that has to be learnt from the experience. It's all too tempting to say, 'Well, it had to happen, therefore it must be OK.' I've learned that to be a completely false and harmful understanding of karma. Instead, I've been shown that if something has to happen (which realistically means everything that's already happened), then I'm beholden not only to feel all the pain of the damage, distress and destructiveness of my actions, but also to look for the deeper reasons behind it and to ask why I might have included that in my script. What is being asked of me? What must I learn?

The script of my life continues to unfold in marvellous and mysterious ways. Each new day is a new turning of the page, which might bring a new character, or a new scene, or announce a new act; or equally, it might force me to stay in a repeated pattern that I've not yet earned the right to move on from. I've come to love the unknowingness of it while also embracing the inevitability of it; and yet more and more I love the prospect that one day, hopefully, I'll have the privilege of seeing it again in its entirety – of feeling again all the highs and lows of life, of meeting my collaborators, of knowing what I did right, of knowing what must be put right, of knowing that it can be put right!

Reclaiming my life, my identity, and my future has been a long, arduous and mostly silent and solitary task. Yet, unlikely though it might seem, I can now look back over my life and feel genuine gratitude for the lessons learnt. Most especially though, I'm grateful to have learnt of the existence of the spiritual entities who once looked upon me with their fierce, unwavering gaze. When I again cross the threshold into the world we call death, I know that they will once more stand majestically before me asking me to account for my life and what I have made of it.

EPILOGUE

Margaret Healy died in 1971 at 77 years of age so her period of time in kamaloca would have ended in 1997. This was the year I first received the impulse to write down this story, when, through the encounter described in the introduction, I obtained confirmation that my memory of the events was more accurate than an 'expert's' interpretation of them.

My father, Frederick Connor, died in 1981 at 52 years of age, so his period of time in kamaloca would have ended in 1998. On reflection, it seems perfectly apt that he should have completed his kamaloca at almost the same time as Margaret Healy. Perhaps this was his way of leaving home again in order to get the midwife.

My brother, Stephen Connor, died in 1991 at 39 years of age, so his kamaloca will end in 2004, the year this book is published. On his deathbed he charged me with the task of making my experiences known.

The ten-year cycle of deaths didn't continue in 2001. Instead, that was the year I was asked by my publisher, Sevak Gulbekian, to write this book.